The Consumer . . . or Else!
Consumer-Centric Business Paradigms

INTERNATIONAL BUSINESS PRESS®

Erdener Kaynak, PhD
Executive Editor

U.S. Trade, Foreign Direct Investments, and Global Competitiveness by Rolf Hackmann

Business Decision Making in China by Huang Quanyu, Joseph Leonard, and Chen Tong

International Management Leadership: The Primary Competitive Advantage by Raimo W. Nurmi and John R. Darling

The Trans-Oceanic Marketing Channel: A New Tool for Understanding Tropical Africa's Export Agriculture by H. Laurens van der Laan

Handbook of Cross-Cultural Marketing by Paul A. Herbig

Guide to Software Export: A Handbook for International Software Sales by Roger Philips

Executive Development and Organizational Learning for Global Business edited by J. Bernard Keys and Robert M. Fulmer

Contextual Management: A Global Perspective by Raghbir (Raj) S. Basi

Japan and China: The Meeting of Asia's Economic Giants by Kazua John Fukuda

Export Savvy: From Basics to Strategy by Zak Karamally

Strategic Networks: The Art of Japanese Interfirm Cooperation by Frank-Jürgen Richter

Export-Import Theory, Practices, and Procedures by Belay Seyoum

Globalization of Business: Practice and Theory by Abbas J. Ali

Internationalization of Companies from Developing Countries by John Kuada and Olav Jull Sørensen

Guanxi: Relationship Marketing in a Chinese Context by Y. H. Wong and Thomas K. P. Leung

Multinational Strategic Management: An Integrative Entrepreneurial Context-Specific Process by Robert J. Mockler

New Product Development: Successful Innovation in the Marketplace by Michael Z. Brooke and William Ronald Mills

Economic Dynamics in Transitional Economies: The Four-P Governments, the EU Enlargement, and the Bruxelles Consensus by Bruno S. Sergi

The Consumer . . . or Else!: Consumer-Centric Business Paradigms by Camille P. Schuster and Donald F. Dufek

The Consumer . . . or Else!

Consumer-Centric Business Paradigms

Camille P. Schuster, PhD
Donald F. Dufek

NEW YORK AND LONDON

First Published by

International Business Press®, an imprint of The Haworth Press, Inc., 10 Alice Street, Binghamton, NY 13904-1580.

Transferred to Digital Printing 2010 by Routledge
270 Madison Ave, New York NY 10016
2 Park Square, Milton Park, Abingdon, Oxon, OX14 4RN

Cover design by Marylouise E. Doyle.

Library of Congress Cataloging-in-Publication Data

Schuster, Camille Passler, 1950-
The consumer . . . or else! : consumer-centric business paradigms / Camille P. Schuster, Donald F. Dufek.
p. cm.
Includes bibliographical references and index.
ISBN 0-7890-1568-4 (hard : alk. paper) — ISBN 0-7890-1569-2 (soft : alk. paper)
1. Consumption (Economics) 2. Customer relations. I. Dufek, Donald F. II. Title.
HC79.C6S265 2003
658.8'12—dc21

2003012040

This book is dedicated to the visionary leaders who had the courage to question existing processes, the vision to see possibilities, and the communication skills to persuade others to try new approaches. The process was not smooth, success was not guaranteed, and everyone was not willing to follow. Those visionaries who had and have the courage to question current assumptions, the stamina to survive the "arrows," and the creativity to design new processes began this transition to a consumer-centered business environment and will lead us into the future.

CONTENTS

ABOUT THE AUTHORS

Camille P. Schuster, PhD, is Full Professor of Marketing at Xavier University. In 1996, Dr. Schuster began to study ECR development activities and has worked with Don Dufek to integrate this information into the MBA curriculum at the university. The initial project focused on integrating ECR activities with the strategic thinking process necessary for guiding organizations to success. In addition, Dr. Schuster has made presentations on this topic to groups of Japanese business people in the food industry, conducted research on this activity among Japanese business people in the food industry, and conducted a seminar on ECR for a consulting group in Australia. Dr. Schuster has published articles in a number of academic journals, such as *Journal of International Consumer Relationship Management, Journal of Public Affairs, Journal of International Marketing, Journal of Global Marketing, Journal of Personal Selling and Sales Management,* and others. In addition, she has co-authored a book with Michael Copeland from Procter & Gamble *(Global Business: Planning for Sales and Negotiation)* that has been well received by both business and academic audiences internationally. Dr. Schuster is also part of the Global Scorecard Committee and has made presentations on this topic at a number of academic meetings. An article on this topic has been included in the book *State of the Art in International Marketing Research,* edited by Dr. Subash Jain at the University of Connecticut.

Don F. Dufek is a retired Senior Vice President and Officer of The Kroger Company. Mr. Dufek was present at the first meeting of trade associations in the grocery and package-goods industry in 1993 to discuss the current state of affairs, competitive situation, and industry threats. Don Dufek and Ralph Drayer, Vice President of Customer Business Development at Procter & Gamble, were co-chairs of the Best Practices Committee that had responsibility for disseminating research findings and knowledge generated by the Joint Industry Council to companies in the industry. In that capacity, they were senior editors of over 40 books on state-of-the-art knowledge as the industry proceeded to incorporate supply chain innovations in the scientific process known as Efficient Consumer Response (ECR). The goal of these ECR activities is to develop a paperless flow of information, continuous product flow, and efficient cash flows to maximize consumer value in as efficient a manner as possible. Since retirement, Mr. Dufek has been asked to speak on this topic at national grocery, food, and package-goods, healthcare, and hardware conferences and companies domestically and at trade association conferences around the world (e.g., Belgium, Spain, Brazil, Australia, Finland, Chile, Argentina, Mexico, and Japan). In addition, Mr. Dufek is an Executive-in-Residence at Xavier University working to integrate these innovations into the business school curriculum, an Advisory Board member at Michigan State University assisting in the development of an integrated curriculum in the food supply industry, and a guest lecturer in the College of Agriculture at Pennsylvania State University. He also teaches MBA students at Ohio State and Xavier University. One of the major points of the message Don brings to all associations and organizations is that ECR is not a project or entity in itself; rather ECR is a group of enabling tools encompassing a new business process that needs to be incorporated into and implemented as an integral part of a company's strategy.

Foreword

"Consumer-Centric Business Paradigms" does not sound like a topic most of us would sit down to explore. But as one starts to understand what that phrase means, we learn that it affects us each day. The buyer/seller landscape is changing. Consumers are in charge of the transactions when we utilize the opportunities open to us and the suppliers provide us the tools. This interesting and well-documented book provides the background and an account of the evolving process of putting the customer in charge.

The Consumer . . . or Else! has tackled the complexity of how this change manifests itself in the worldwide marketplace. First the authors explore the recent landscape for signs of robust change, then clarify how the selection, distribution, and payment of goods and services can be accomplished having given the purchaser full knowledge of availability, quality, and price. Through many examples, this book makes clear this is not a "grocery store phone-in concept," but a huge capacity enlargement covering a myriad of products and services. This change affects at least as much the sellers as the buyers, as Katherine Lemon of Harvard University (*MMR* February 19, 2001) points out:

> Retailers must understand their customers better because the balance of power has shifted to the consumer, who expects more and will tolerate less frustration and disappointment. The customer is changing the shopping experience.

This book supplies a fine early example of putting the consumer first. Wal-Mart and Kmart started even, one store each in 1962. Sam Walton's approach was to create added value through continually improving efficiency and sharing gains with Wal-Mart's customers. In 2000, Kmart had sales of $37 billion, Wal-Mart $167.8 billion. Walton and his successors tough-minded, consistent push toward better efficient practices resulted in savings that were shared with customers. Technology played but a subservient role initially in launching this retail giant that remains an early beacon in a new way of putting customers first, an approach consumers recognized and continue to support.

Efficient Consumer Response (ECR) arose to become a different approach to serving the customer better. The food industry in the 1980s and early 1990s was divided into two warring camps, suppliers and wholesalers/retailers, neither spending much energy in cooperating on behalf of the customer. Encouraged by the result of cooperation twenty years earlier on the Universal Product Identification Code (UPC), ECR got substantial support from all related trade associations. These efforts have now allowed, through will, cooperation, and technology, retail customers across the globe a growing share of control over what, where, how, and at what price their purchase of a wide variety of products will be made.

These two examples are fundamental to the understanding of the current progress toward a one-marketplace world. The supply side in many industries has continued to expand its ability to source cooperatively worldwide while the Internet becomes a local outlet as a place to shop. Wal-Mart is now significantly involved in this technology utilization while traditional markets benefit by the clearer recognition that their success is not tightly bound to store proximity. Change is everywhere. As the authors point out:

> Customers demand more than just a fair price. Price is an issue, but only one part of today's value equation. Convenience, location, price, quality, and service are all part of the consumer value equation.

To operate on a potentially worldwide basis for some firms and for others a nonlocalized and still expanded ability to reach more sourcing alternatives, the business, whether retail, wholesale, manufacturing, or service needs current technology, enablers to use the tools, and then integration with the balance of the supply chain to execute the transaction. Section III develops these links with sufficient detail to allow the reader to understand how big as well as how important this integrated task is. Using the Internet is one step; effective integration with adjoining links in the supply chain to the customer is quite another. For instance, with 30,000 new SKUs and 2,000 alone in the U.S. grocery and packaged goods business, and between 80 to 90 percent gone in eighteen months, the problems of cost as well as keeping up are complex for all parties. And just keeping up is not sufficient; "forging ahead" is expected.

Staples has concentrated on integration, reports Tim Hanrahan in *The Wall Street Journal Europe* (May 2, 2003): "Customers can buy from Staples catalog, stores or web site and . . . each is designed to serve as a sales pitch and back up for the others." Pricing is also integrated and delivery on orders over $50 and returns can be made for online purchases at the store. "Since its stores have been slimmed down to focus on higher margin items aimed at businesses, Staples web outpost has become all the more important for finding items that aren't in stock." The results have been gratifying. "Revenues rose 30% to $11.6 billion in year ended 2/01/02 from $8.9 billion in 2000."

This internal integration must connect externally to utilize the breadth and strength of the supply chain. If, as the authors suggest, "the business change process is 80 percent people and only 20 percent technology," not only systems and software, but willing collaboration is required, trained to think in new ways to solve old problems. At Borders Group, Hanrahan relates, "customers have a high tendency to search for information online and then purchase in store" as well as search in store and purchase online. Borders had the capacity to serve the New York customer but Amazon, its major competitor, was much better situated to deliver nationally. "Go to Borders.com today and you end up at an Amazon page with the Borders logo uptop." This is surely integration that serves the customers and preserves a buyer's loyalty but introduces each to a competitive source. Borders made the choice that serving the customer comes first.

There is also in Section III a fine discussion of tools, processes that make them useful, and examples of collaboration similar to the previous. If you are interested in becoming a player in this new world of customers first, in Section IV, you will be encouraged by the twelve varied companies that have moved in that direction in major ways. Most are not, and perhaps never will be, all the way to customer first as described by the authors, but the advantages to staying as you are appear clearly to be shrinking as the various industries accept the challenge and opportunity. The choice is yours—but on second thought, the choice is your customer's.

In the closing paragraph of the preface to *Revolution at the Checkout Counter* Stephen A. Brown wrote:

> If we can understand how the grocery industry came together and looked beyond the narrow corporate interests to devise something that both improved productivity and enhanced competition within the industry, we might find a model for future endeavors. Such is my hope.

That first major cooperative move by the U.S. grocery sector has provided not only a key element in the integration process but, as well, an outstanding model of how to work together for the common good.

David Jenkins

Preface

Today's business environment is and has been in turmoil. Companies such as Kmart, Enron, WorldCom, Fleming, United, Guidant, and Dynegy are embroiled in controversy, bankruptcy, or mergers and acquisitions. Where's the focus—on CEO compensation, government regulations, worldwide political problems, expense reductions, employee cutbacks, or the consumer? Everyone says the "Consumer is #1," but most companies live a different vision.

This book is based on two perspectives. One is a warning to business leaders that the old business models are broken and the need to change is paramount to **SURVIVAL**! Two is a demonstration to academia of the changing business processes that must be incorporated into the education of business students, particularly MBAs.

Despite the complexity of application, the proposition is simply stated. We are talking about changing the business process—changing the way product flows, the way information flows, and the way cash flows. These processes literally change the way raw material is sourced, the way product is manufactured, the way it is transported, the way it is bought and sold, and the way it is presented to the consumer.

A great deal of our writing relates to the food industry; however, the change propositions relate to most businesses as evidenced by the applications in the mass merchant industry, the food industry, the health care industry, the hardware industry, and the food service industry. The book portrays **WHY** change is necessary along with **WHAT** needs to be done, and **HOW** to do it successfully. The authors have traveled to more than 20 countries, working with companies and countries, helping to establish these new business models.

Competitive advantage comes to those companies embracing this new business model, applying the new processes, training and educating their associates to this new way, and then measuring and rewarding this new behavior. Business life cycles are shorter and product life cycles are shrinking rapidly. Consumers are constantly being bombarded by new formats. Companies are finding more cost effective, more efficient ways to go to market and constantly adding **VALUE** to the consumer.

Bankruptcies and business failures are an everyday occurrence. "Business as usual" is doomed to failure and companies which refuse to adopt change and provide added **VALUE** will simply not be here in the future. We strongly believe that those companies which do not change . . . those which do not subscribe to this value added thesis, will not survive! Thus, the title of our book, *The Consumer . . . or Else!*

Acknowledgments

Many people were directly and indirectly involved in making this book possible. Over 350 businesspeople were involved in the original Efficient Consumer Response (ECR) Committee, the Best Practices Committee, and the Global Commerce Initiative. Many more are involved in collaborative activities throughout many industries. The efforts and learnings of all these people provide the foundation for this book. Their pilot tests, failures, and successes point the way of the future for all of us.

Xavier University supported the effort with a sabbatical. Students at both Xavier University and Arizona State University—East have shared their insights and learning as they work in the industry, conduct research, and share their insights in class. The staff at The Haworth Press worked hard to create a unique format for the book that challenges the status quo.

We sincerely thank everyone who contributed to this effort.

Section I: Rationale

"[I]f you were hoping for a return to business as usual, forget it . . . once docile consumers have awakened to their new powers."

BusinessWeek OnLine
March 23, 2001

Historically, power struggles raged between suppliers and distributors. Recently, both parties awakened to the fact that neither of them has the ultimate power—it now resides solely with the consumer!

Consumers search magazines, online Web sites, and talk with others to find out about products and services: the quality, the price, the specifications, the differences. When ready to purchase they can visit a retail outlet, order over the phone or via fax, or order online from the manufacturer, broker, intermediary, Internet provider, or distributor. To receive the product consumers can pick it up or can have it delivered to their home or office.

Consumers have more information available to them than ever before and, consequently, are more demanding and more specific regarding their expectations. When making purchases, consumers do not have to be constrained to only the outlets within ten to fifteen miles. If consumers are not satisfied with the service or product, they can choose another product or source.

Consumers have choices and they exercise those choices. Companies used to work toward selling TO consumers. Now they need to reorient themselves to retaining valuable consumers.

This section of the book describes why a change in thinking is required, what demassification of the consumer market means, and includes a caveat to remember that business takes place in a global environment.

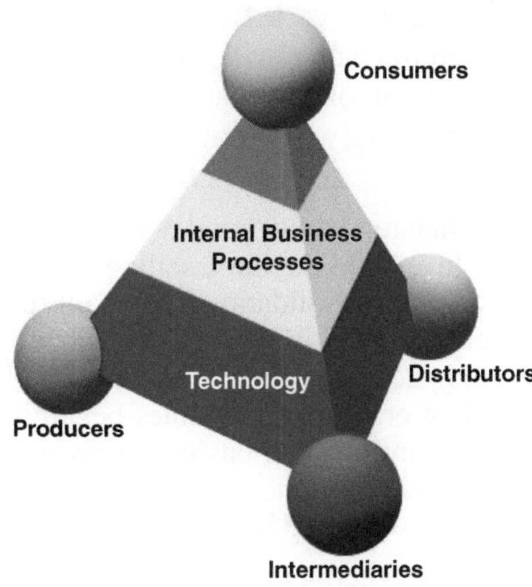

Chapter 1

What's Going On?

"Revolution, says Webster's, is 'a sudden, radical or complete change . . . a basic reorientation.' To anyone in the world of business, that sounds about right. We all sense that the changes surrounding us are not mere trends but the workings of large, unruly forces: the globalization of markets; the spread of information technology and computer networks; the dismantling of hierarchy, the structure that has essentially organized work since the mid-19th century."

Thomas Stewart
"Welcome to the Revolution," 1993

The title of the book, *The Consumer . . . or Else!,* dramatically and simply states the reality of business today —recognize that the **consumer** solely possesses the power in today's marketplace. The supplier, distributor, manufacturer, retailer, or intermediary who fails to recognize this basic fact will be doomed to failure and will not survive! The business process is changing—changing the way product flows, the way information flows, and the way cash flows. The companies that recognize this need to change will hold huge competitive advantages, and the companies that fail to adopt these new business processes simply will not be here in the future! Read on . . .

"In many respects, the last 5 years felt like a recession. No food inflation, no ability to raise prices and a tight labor market while trying to improve productivity."

Ed Comeau, Vice President, Donaldson, Lufkin & Jenrette, *Progressive Grocer,* March 1999

Companies do not change without good reason. The number of restructurings, leveraged buyouts, selling off of divisions or products, mergers, consolidations, and bankruptcies suggest that a lot of change is taking place. Dot-com companies emerged at a rapid pace and increased in value with tremendous speed and then crashed. Companies began selling off specific brands to streamline their business activities or to focus on growth opportunities. "Brick and click" companies merged. Why so much movement? **SURVIVAL!**

Doing business in today's economy and surviving requires a new paradigm. What is at the center of this new approach to doing business? **CONSUMERS!** Consumers not only demand higher quality and lower prices but also expect convenient, quick, customized service. They expect in-stock conditions and quality. They demand value and respect. Companies grow larger but need to act like start-ups in terms of speed to provide unique value to consumers. Global markets mean large numbers of consumers, but these consumers want to be treated as individuals, and the mass market no longer exists.

"[T]he consumer and the marketplace are very unforgiving for the inefficient—even more unforgiving for the ineffective."

Daniel Wegman, President, Wegman's Food and Co-Chair ECR Executive Committee, *ECR Focus,* May 12, 1997

Companies in industries from financial services to groceries to consumer goods to health care to hardware to automobiles are adopting these new business processes and winning in the marketplace. Their competitors are falling by the wayside. If you think, analogously, about movement to this new paradigm as a highway, about a third of the companies are on the new superhighway, moving rapidly, enjoying success, and employing best practices, while keeping their eyes open for bumps, barriers, and the other players on the highway. Another third of the companies are on the entrance ramp. They have seen the success of those on the highway, would like to be part of that group, and are making the first steps to moving their companies in that direction, trying to merge onto this new superhighway. Getting up-to-speed in the fundamental processes is necessary before merging onto the superhighway and driving in the fast lanes. The last third of the companies are watching this new process, are not sure this route would be successful for them, do not recognize the need for change, have not started to revamp their business processes, and will be left behind forever, lost on the back country roads.

The companies on the new superhighway have made a commitment to this new consumer-centric business process, have demonstrated success using this route, are developing competitive, collaborative strategies to keep them ahead of the other companies on the highway, and are speeding ahead of those on the entrance ramp or those refusing to get on the highway. They will be the winners and the survivors!

The model on the cover and at the beginning of each chapter illustrates the consumer-centric paradigm that reflects the changes made by successful companies. Industry players (suppliers, retailers, and intermediaries) use technology to coordinate internal business processes and facilitate collaborative business practices, processes, and procedures to create efficient supply chains and consumer value. While companies have always considered consumers' needs, the new business paradigm demands that consumers' needs and wants be placed at the center of all internal and collaborative business activities. This is definitely a sea change in the way companies operate.

The purpose of this book is to examine this new direction and provide suggestions for success in this new consumer-centric business world. The first three chapters of the book set the scene by describing major factors that are shaping the current business environment, consumer reorientation, and global perspectives. The second three chapters of the book examine this new consumer-centric approach from the perspective of suppliers, intermediaries, and retailers as well as the business processes being used to create more efficient supply chains and more effective demand fulfillment processes. The third group of three chapters focuses on tools that are used to implement this new business paradigm in the areas of technology, internal business processes, and collaboration. The fourth group of two chapters provides examples of success and answers frequently asked questions.

FACTORS SHAPING TODAY'S MARKETPLACE

This section identifies some of the factors motivating companies to get on this new superhighway. There must be some compelling reason(s) or common enemies to convince companies of the need to take this new road. **SO . . . WHY CHANGE?**

Alternative Formats

Over the past fifty years, consumers no longer have had to visit a store or work with a sales representative face-to-face to make a purchase or sign a contract. With the advent of the credit card, purchase order, or bank transfer, infomercials ask consumers to dial a 1-800 number, catalog order forms are mailed or faxed, and orders are transmitted over the Internet. As a result, consumers no longer have to sit down face-to-face with a salesperson or visit a store to make purchases. Physical location is no longer a major barrier or advantage to doing business. The business proposition is no longer "How do you get the consumer to come to the goods?" but, rather, "How do you get the goods to the consumer?"

Technology

Catalogs, company home pages on the Internet, portals, or intermediaries provide product comparison information from the comfort of home, also eliminating the need to travel from store to store to gather information. The number of computers in consumers' homes, offices, schools, and universities has increased dramatically over the past ten years. Nielsen/NetRatings reports that 429 million people have Internet access around the world.[1] About a quarter of European households, a third of households in Asia Pacific, and about half of American households have Internet access. The number of PCs in the home in Europe and Asia Pacific is continuing to grow at a fast pace and a large proportion of them are connecting to the Internet. One impact of this trend is that Americans will not dominate Internet usage for much longer and English might not even be the dominant language of the Internet in the future.

With about 30 percent of the U.S. workforce traveling out of the office, the demand for portable devices is high. The number of cell phones, pagers, Web devices, and personal digital assistants has increased at double-digit figures for several years. Nokia, Yankee Group, and Lehman Brothers all predicted that there would be 420 to 450 million handsets worldwide in 2002.[2] One impact of the increasing use of handheld sets is the ability to stay connected while mobile. Consumers are not tied to a particular location, creating distribution challenges; a broader range of competitors emerge for local retail outlets; and consumers can be connected to work or family at any time of day.

If location is not a barrier, the possibility of global commerce becomes a reality for companies of any size. With only 5 percent of the world's population in the United States and a slow-growing domestic market, U.S. companies have seen potential growth opportunities in other countries. Businesses in other countries that have even smaller percentages of the worldwide population see the United States as an attractive market. By linking electronically, companies are able to develop systems that facilitate inventory management and purchasing activities. Connectivity has broken the location barrier.

"One out of every four dollars spent in U.S. supermarkets reportedly occurs in a store owned by a foreign, usually European chain."

Tracy Mullin, CEO, National Retail Federation, *Chain Store Age,* Oct. 2000

Changing Demographics

The aging of the population in developed countries provides an emphasis on healthy living—nutrition, vitamins, alternative therapies, and physical fitness. With the increase in the number of women working, more organized activities for children, and an emphasis on continuing education, consum-

"3 out of 5 women are in the workforce."

Willard N. Ander Jr., *Retailing's New Frontier,* Dec. 1998

ers are stressed about having enough time to address increasing demands. They are continuously saying, "Don't waste my time!"

"Retailers must understand their customers better because the balance of power has shifted to the consumer, who expects more and will tolerate less frustration and disappointment. The customer is changing the shopping experience."

Katherine Lemon, Harvard University, *MMR,* Feb. 19, 2001

Consumer expectations continue to change with increasing demands for high quality products and services, a desire that individual needs be met, reasonable prices, and deliveries occurring in a timely manner.[3] At the same time consumers demand fair prices and to be treated as individuals. Products and services are available in many locations from many providers. Consumers have many choices and they vote with their wallets. Those companies that recognize the trends, change accordingly, and offer consumers what they want will survive.

Company Responses

If a particular company decides not to change and not to get on the new superhighway, another company will meet the consumers' needs and take the business away. From 1976 to 2000, the grocery industry's "share of stomach" changed significantly (see Table 1.1). The total weekly grocery expense fell slightly from $92 dollars spent per week in 1996 to $91 spent per week in 2001. In addition, the food service industry took billions of dollars of revenue from the grocery industry simply because the grocery industry failed to recognize the changing consumer trends.[4] For example, the initial success of Boston Market was phenomenal. By offering home-cooked meals, Boston Market made it possible for consumers to serve nutritious, traditional hot meals with little preparation time. As a result, consumers frequented Boston Market and other businesses serving prepared meals while purchasing fewer groceries. The "Category Killer" stores, such as Boston Market, Drug Emporium, and PETsMART, have been successful by appealing to customers with specific products and services that fit their lifestyles and changing needs. Predictions estimate that the food service industry will attract 62 percent of the $123 billion in new food spending by 2010 and retail food operators will capture only 38 percent of the new growth.[5]

"Just three years ago Boston Market and Kenny Rogers Roasters were ranked #1 and #2 respectively. Both have since filed for Chapter 11."

Take Out Business, Nov. 15, 1998

TABLE 1.1. Share of Stomach

	1976 (%)	1986 (%)	2000 (%)
Food service	38	43	50
Grocery	62	57	50

Source: Alva, Marilyn (2001), "Grocers Meet Changes in Tastes," *Investor's Business Daily* (October 15), p. A14; Dobbin, Ben (1996), "Shoppers Park Their Grocery Carts and Eat a Little Dinner," *Marketing News* (May 20), p. 10.

The U.S. automobile industries ignored the predictions of a gasoline shortage in the early 1970s and/or refused to believe that U.S. consumers would change their purchasing behavior from large gas-guzzling automobiles to small, fuel-efficient cars. The U.S. automobile manufacturers saw their share of automobile production fall from 97 percent in 1979 to 82 percent in 1990, while the share of new car sales from imports and foreign automobile manufacturers in the United States grew from 22 percent in 1979 to 41 percent in 1990.[6] The Japanese companies that recognized the potential impact of a gasoline shortage and changing consumer sentiment produced small, fuel-efficient cars and took thousands of consumers away from the U.S. companies of General Motors, Chrysler, and Ford.

"A part of the change occurring in the packaged goods industry is being driven by forces common to all industries. Communication and transportation lower barriers between countries, causing global competition to grow. The spread of information technology eliminates the need for middle managers. As layers of hierarchy are removed, organizations must become more flexible and responsive."

Barbara Kahn and Leigh McAlister, *Grocery Revolution,* 1997, p. 7

In 1962 the Kresge company opened its first Kmart discount department store; at the same time, Wal-Mart opened its first store. By 1985 Kmart was growing faster than Wal-Mart (Table 1.2). In 1989 Kmart was the largest discount retailer. By 1994 Kmart was still growing domestically, and also had 147 stores outside the United States in Canada, Mexico, Czech Republic, Slovakia, and Singapore. However, even with this growth, by 1994 Kmart's sales were only about half of Wal-Mart's sales (Table 1.3). Wal-Mart also began international expansion in the mid-1990s and by 1995 was the largest retailer in the world. By the end of 1996, Kmart had closed all of its stores outside of North America and Wal-Mart had 298 stores outside the United States. By January 2001, Wal-Mart had more stores domestically and a domestic revenue that was two-thirds larger than Kmart's. That figure does not include the revenue generated in the additional 1,014 stores outside the United States. Beginning in the mid-1990s Wal-Mart began to outdistance Kmart and has not stopped.[7] Wal-Mart was changing the business process, creating added value for the consumer through improved efficiencies, while Kmart was struggling with focus and identity.

Wal-Mart is one of the companies on the superhighway, having adopted many new business practices and processes. With a strong consumer orientation, Wal-Mart offers consumers products they want at prices they are willing to pay. In

TABLE 1.2. Number of Stores

	1962	1989	1994	2000
Kmart	1	2,180	2,316	2,105
Wal-Mart	1	827	1,967	2,624 3,642*

Source: "A Retailing Legend Is Born," Kmart History at <www.Kmart.com>, August 22, 2001; Donlon, J.P. (1995), "A Glass Act," *Chief Executive* (July), No. 105, pp. 40-49; Kmart's Annual Report (1994); Kmart's Annual Report 2000 (ending December 31, 2000) at <www.Kmart.com>; Wal-Mart's Annual Report (1994); Wal-Mart's 2001 Annual Report (ending January 31, 2001) at <www.Wal-Mart.com>; Walker, Richard (1985), "Kmart 1985 Profits Decline 56 Per Cent to $221 Million," *Business News* (August 19), Reuters.

*This is the number of stores worldwide.

TABLE 1.3. Revenue in Billions of Dollars

	1989	1994	2000
Kmart	22.9	34.1	37.0
Wal-Mart	16.8	77.8	164.8

Source: "State of the Industry" (1995), *Chain Store Age Executive* (August), pp. 3A, 78; Annual Report (2001), Wal-Mart, <www.Wal-Mart.com>; Annual Report (2000), Kmart, <www.Kmart.com>.

addition, Wal-Mart created new back-office practices, collaborative relationships with suppliers, and more efficient distribution systems, all of which created more efficient operations (Figure 1.1). With business practices that continually reduce SG&A expenses and by continuing to invest in products and processes that allow Wal-Mart to offer consumers what they want, when they want it, at a price they are willing to pay, Wal-Mart has consistently kept its costs down and passed the savings on to the consumer.

WHAT'S WRONG WITH THE OLD PARADIGM?

There is something wrong when $50 billion is spent in the grocery industry in promotion and deal dollars, and manufacturers do not think they are getting their money's worth and retailers/distributors do not think they are getting their fair share.

"The grocery channel spent . . . 13% of sales—on trade promotion."

Glen Terbeek, *Agentry Agenda,* 1999

More importantly, there is something wrong when very little of this $50 billion gets to the consumers.

There is something wrong when technology simply replaces existing systems/procedures rather than being used to re-create the business process to gain efficiencies.

	1985	1986	1987	1988	1989	1990	1991	1992	1993	1994	1995	1996	1997
Gross Profit Rate (%)	26.2	24.7	24.0	23.0	22.2	22.2	21.8	20.7	20.4	20.6	20.5%	20.4	20.2
Expense Rate (%)	19.2	18.2	17.6	17.0	16.5	16.3	16.3	15.8	15.6	14.7	15.1	15.7	15.6

FIGURE 1.1. Wal-Mart's Expense and Profit Rates (*Source:* Reprinted by permission from *Chain Store Age* [May 1998]. Copyright Lebhar-Friedman, Inc., 425 Park Avenue, New York, NY 10022.)

There is something wrong when all entities fend for themselves versus recognizing the power and the value of synergistic business practices by collaborating for success.

"94% of the top 100 department store chains of 1969 are gone now."

Peter Gertler, Deloitte Consulting, *MMR,* Feb. 21, 2000

Most companies do not notice a threat until their revenues or profits begin falling. By then, other companies using new business processes have taken their consumers and market share away. Many of the companies who elected to stay on the back roads are no longer in existence. For example, in the grocery industry six of the stores on the top ten list in 1970 were not even on the list by 2000 (see Table 1.4). Wal-Mart did not begin food operations until 1965 but was number one in 2000. Fighting back against these strong competitors on the new superhighway is difficult, if not impossible.

"At the end of the day, they (consumers) want more value, quality products, good services in a shopping environment that has more than low prices. Price competition is diminishing as motivation to shop a store."

Ed Comeau, Vice President, Donaldson, Lufkin & Jenrette, *Progressive Grocer,* March 1999

You have to know your consumers, stay in touch with their changing needs, and design business practices to make it easy for consumers to do business with you. You must be an efficient, low-cost operator to be able to offer products at a reasonable price and be a low priced merchant! If you don't, someone else will! Just ask Wal-Mart, Boston Market, Montgomery Ward, Toyota, Kmart, Food Fair, or Jewel.

Just doing more marketing or consumer research will not keep you out of the Valley of the Damned.[8] Today, consum-

TABLE 1.4. Top Ten Supermarkets in the United States

1970s	1980s	1990s	2000
A&P	Safeway	Kroger	Wal-Mart
Safeway	Kroger	American	Kroger
Kroger	A&P	Safeway	Albertson's
Food Fair	American	A&P	Safeway
Acme	Winn-Dixie	Winn-Dixie	Ahold
Jewel	Lucky	Albertson's	SuperValu
Lucky	Grand Union	Food Lion	Fleming
National Tea	Albertson's	Publix	Winn-Dixie
Winn-Dixie	Jewel	Ahold	Delhaize
Grand Union	SGC	Vons	A&P

Source: Food Trends and Industry Futures Workshop (1996), Andersen Consulting, December 5.

ers have access to more information about products and services, can choose the form of delivery they desire, can purchase the product from one of any number of sources, and can do this at any time of day or night. Consumers can easily begin purchasing from another source rather than return to your company. Therefore, companies need to be consumer-centric and sensitive to changing needs in this dynamic marketplace.

Consumer-centric means that all front-office and back-office activities are focused around the consumers, making it easy for consumers to place orders, ask questions, voice complaints or make suggestions, track deliveries, return items, or find information. Delivery systems need to make these products and services available when and where consumers want to purchase them and change from a "push" based marketing system to a "pull" based replenishment system based on consumption. Using these systems companies can learn about their consumers, track changing needs, and develop new products or services that consumers want at affordable, fair prices.

"Change is not merely necessary to life . . . it is life."

Alvin Toffler

Companies that ignore this new paradigm do so at their own peril. You are competing with those companies that have already made it to the new superhighway and those that are on the entrance ramp poised to join the race. You can lag behind and watch your competitors win or you can make consumers the center of your business activity.

If interviewed, most companies would readily admit, "Of course, the consumer is Number 1!", but, in practice, other priorities and business activities dominate the core business practices. It is easy to get caught up in the "activity trap," concentrating on accounting, finance, analyst meetings, union negotiations, etc., and lose sight of what you are doing to **add value** for your consumers. If you don't add value for consumers, someone else will and you will lose. The issue is survival!

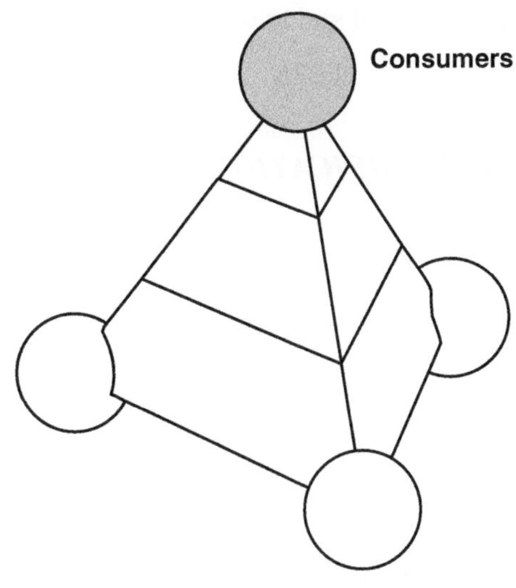

Chapter 2

Changing Consumers

"We cannot solve today's problems with the same level of thinking that created the problem in the first place."

Albert Einstein

Are customers really so different? They still purchase food, buy homes or rent apartments, spend money on entertainment, pay for utilities, purchase furnishings, buy clothing, and purchase electronic items. The amount of overall spending has risen as the population has increased. So what's different? **Demassification.** In *Future Shock,* Alvin Toffler coined the word "demassification" and explained that the social fabric would begin to pull apart as the population splintered into small groups.

"The manufacturers used to have the power, then the power shifted to the retailers and now the power is shifting to the consumer."

Natan Tabak, Senior Vice President, Wakefern, *Executive Technology,* March 2000

As the consumer market splinters into small groups, traditional mass marketing practices are not effective. To succeed in this environment, companies must analyze the fragmentation of markets, examine changing consumer needs, and find ways to provide customized products and services. How are markets becoming demassified and how does that affect consumers' needs?

DEMASSIFICATION

Traditional Families

In 1960, 80 percent of households were composed of families (one or two parents with kids). By 2000, only 68 percent were family households; 52 percent were a married couple with a family; 23.5 percent were in a household with their own children; 12 percent of households were headed by a woman with no husband present; 7 percent headed a household with their own children; and 32 percent of households were classified as "non-family" households.[1] Obviously, the image of a nuclear family unit (mother and/or father with their own children) with traditional purchasing habits does not fit many of today's family units or households. These new household configurations have their own unique purchasing habits.

Working Parents

In 1960, 23 percent of adult women were in the workforce; in 2000, 60 percent of adult women were in the workforce. Of all adults who have children, 90 percent are in the labor force.[2] With so many parents working, time is at a premium. Convenience, healthy choices, prices, and time required for the tasks involved are all important criteria when these consumers are choosing products and services.

Diversity

Not only are minority groups growing in size in the United States, but also there is great diversity among the minority groups. About 12.5 percent of the total population is Hispanic or Latino: 58.5 percent of that group are Mexican,

9.6 percent are Puerto Rican, 3.5 percent are Cuban, and 28.4 percent are from other countries. While only 3.6 percent of the total U.S. population is Asian, they represent a number of different countries and ethnic groups: 23.8 percent are Chinese, 18.1 percent are Filipino, 16.4 percent are Asian Indian, 10.9 percent are Vietnamese, 10.5 percent are Korean, 7.8 percent are Japanese, and 12.5 percent are from other Asian countries. Hispanics or Asians cannot be targeted as a single minority group. These groups are really composed of smaller fragmented groups, each with its own needs for products and services.

Language Spoken at Home

Not all people in the United States speak English on a regular basis. About 18 percent of people over the age of five speak a language other than English at home: 12.5 percent speak Spanish at home, 3.7 percent speak an Indo-European language besides Spanish at home, and 2.7 percent speak Asian or Pacific Islander languages at home.[3] The variety of languages and values among these ethnic groups creates a number of different, very small target markets, each with its own distinct set of needs.

Spending Habits

The U.S. population is not one homogenous "melting pot" with similar values, preferences, tastes, or purchasing habits. The needs of this market not only are fragmented but also do not remain constant over time. Not surprisingly, spending habits changed considerably over the ten-year period between 1987 and 1997.[4]

- Spending Increases:
  +20 percent in education
  +15 percent in health care
  +13 percent in personal care products and services
  + 8 percent in entertainment
  + 5 percent in housing

- Spending Decreases:
  –25 percent on major appliances
  –24 percent on alcoholic beverages
  –18 percent on newspapers, books, and magazines
  –15 percent on clothing
  – 3 percent on food

As the market becomes more fragmented, as consumers enter new phases of their lives, as the environment changes, so, too, do purchasing habits change. Knowing what products and services are important to consumer groups **TODAY** is critical for success.

Life Cycles

Baby Boomers have had a significant impact on the economy throughout their lifetime. Now they are beginning to enter the "AARP" group (fifty plus). Some have young children; some are empty nesters; some are single; some have adult children living with them; some have grandchildren living with them. Health concerns may be similar across members of the group because of their similarity in age, but spending habits are not necessarily similar because of their different living conditions. The Baby Boomlet group is either in college or entering the workforce. This is the first generation introduced to computers as they were growing up. Some are extremely techno-literate, demanding the newest and latest gadgets; some are not as techno-literate and need "easy-to-use" gadgets. Members of the group may have some things in common, such as age, but their life conditions are not necessarily the same. As a result, change in spending habits will be more dynamic and more pronounced in the marketplace.

Seniors and Entertainment Spending

Householders in the sixty-five to seventy-four age group spent more on entertainment in 1997 than households headed by someone under the age of twenty-five. Entertainment spending by households headed by someone sixty-five or older increased faster than any other age group during the ten-year period from 1987 to 1997. Households headed by someone seventy-five years of age or more spent 98 percent more on entertainment in 1997 than in 1987.[5] Seniors, who are healthy, have disposable incomes and are active, travel, go to movies, play sports, square dance, ski, and eat out often. Their life circumstances differ from those of senior citizens of ten and twenty years ago. Their product and service needs are also different.

Generation X

Xer's (those born between 1965 and 1978) are a diverse group with a "been there, done that" perspective. This group is entering the years of household formation when most purchases are for the household and family. Since Xer's get bored quickly, they don't spend much time doing any one thing; they are interested in what's new, what hasn't been done before, and what's entertaining. Both image and in-store merchandising are important to this group because 80 percent of them make purchase decisions at the point-of-purchase.[6] While this group may have needs similar to past generations who have been in a similar life cycle stage of creating households and beginning families, their choice of products and services, as well as their process of decision making, is distinctly different.

Computer Technology

In 1997 the average household spent more on computer technology than on major appliances, lawn and gardening, or housewares. The highest spending groups were households headed by someone between the ages of forty-five and fifty-four who spent 61 percent more on computer technology in 1997 than in 1987. The second highest group spending money on technology were households headed by someone between the ages of thirty-five and forty-four. The third largest group were householders between the ages of fifty-five and sixty-four; these people spend more on computer technology than householders between the ages of twenty-five and thirty-four.[7] Not just young people are buying computers or high-tech gadgets. Some adults purchase computers so their children can do homework; some purchase computers so they can work at home in the evenings; some buy products to create home offices; some buy pagers so their "latchkey" children can contact them in emergencies; some buy pagers so their teenagers can stay in touch with friends; and some buy personal digital assistants to organize their hectic schedules. Spending on technology has increased, but the money was not necessarily spent for the same items or for the same reasons.

Food Spending

Not only was there a 3 percent decrease in spending for food consumed at home, but also there was a 13 percent decrease in spending on food consumed away from home. However, there was a 61 percent increase in the amount of money spent on take-out dinners.[8] People are definitely not cooking at home as much as in the past, but they may still be eating at home. Nutritious food in convenient formats, like Boston Market, new meal solutions at grocery stores, or companies that provide gourmet dinners for pick-up or delivery are a big hit with today's consumers.

Shopping Time

During the 1980s consumers, on average, visited the mall three times a month, staying for twelve hours each month and visiting seven stores. By the 1990s that changed to visiting the mall about two times a month and visiting three and a half stores.[9] Time is a precious commodity and less of it is spent on traditional mall shopping. One study found that 40 percent of consumers do not know at 4 p.m. what they're going to have for dinner that night and that 60 percent of afternoon planners don't know what they're going to buy when they walk in the door of the store.[10] Knowing where and how these people shop is critical for attracting their business.

Home As a Haven

During the 1990s consumers began spending more money on their homes for exercise and entertainment equipment, safety products, and storage solutions.[11] For instance, consumers have increased purchases of smoke detectors, carbon monoxide detectors, water purification systems, and various types of exercise equipment to improve the safety of their homes or their health. VCRs, big screen televisions, DVDs, and surround-sound systems have been selling well, providing at-home alternatives for entertainment. This style of home entertainment can provide quality family time, relaxation after the stresses of a hectic work week, or a friendly environment for sharing time with friends.

While the total amount of money being spent has grown, major shifts in spending have occurred that correlate with changing demographics, changing lifestyles, changing life cycle patterns, and concerns about the economy. As a result, old assumptions about how consumers make purchases do not apply. Because more parents are working, because seniors are in better health and have saved money, because computer technology has expanded rapidly, criteria for decision making and the type of purchases made by specific groups have shifted. Consumers may belong to different target segments depending upon the products being purchased. While people of a certain age may have similar health concerns and purchase similar products, the same people who form this group may have very different entertainment and technology needs. While people in one age group may spend a similar amount of money on technology, they may purchase different products to satisfy different needs. While one group of people may be purchasing similar entertainment products, they may be buying it for very different needs.

"Today's retail industry must face one truly significant reality—the consumer is in charge. Consumers enjoy more choice than ever before and have access to an ever-increasing amount of information upon which to base their buying decisions. Consumers today are very sophisticated and have a clear understanding of value."

Theresa Williams, Indiana University, Mark J. Larson, KPMG

Consumers must now be viewed as **multidimensional,** which means they are part of different target groups at different times depending upon the product or service. In other words, they are a moving target with changing affiliations and changing needs.

CONSUMER VALUE EQUATION

By the mid-1990s a shift in consumer criteria for purchase decisions was already taking place. Data from the Kurt Salmon Associates study of the food industry indicated that only 51 percent of consumers surveyed identified price as their most important reason for making a grocery purchase. About 49 percent of the consumers chose other criteria as being more important. In general, 91 percent of consumers put cleanliness/neatness of the store on their list, 90 percent put quality produce, 88 percent added quality meat, 82 percent listed courteous employees, 78 percent added low price, and 77 percent indicated that convenient location was an important criterion.[12]

The Food Marketing Institute (FMI) tracked consumers' reasons for choosing a store and found that they change (see Table 2.1). In 1995, 97 percent of consumers agreed that price was important, while 77 percent agreed that low price was very important in 1997.[13] Other factors, like Clean Neat Store or Quality Produce or Courteous Friendly Employees or Accurate Shelf Tags, were more important. Another study of consumers found that while 30 percent of the consumers chose price as being most important, 24 percent chose variety/assortment, and 23 percent chose convenient location.[14] Consumers' criteria for choosing a particular store do change over time and price was only one factor in their value equation.

"[I]f you were hoping for a return to business as usual, forget it . . . once docile consumers have awakened to their new powers."

BusinessWeek Online, March 23, 2001

When consumers relied upon cars or mass transportation to reach retail outlets, convenience meant physical proximity. Now convenience means much more—one-stop shopping, longer hours for two-career families, and a good in-stock track record.[15] Even the old real estate slogan of "location, location, location" is not as important today as it once was. Satisfaction with customer service and construction quality drove 70 percent of home buyers' overall satisfaction; location of the house accounted for only 3 percent of their evaluation.[16] In addition, many consumers research products over the Internet whether they purchase online or in a local retail outlet. Consumers using the Internet are not restricted to the

TABLE 2.1. Reasons for Picking a Store

	% Saying Very or Somewhat Important		
Reasons	**1997**	**1996**	**1995**
Clean, neat store	91	91	99
High-quality produce	91	90	99
High-quality meat	86	88	94
Courteous, friendly employees	82	82	96
Use before/sell-by date marked	82	–	–
Accurate shelf tags	77	–	–
Low prices	77	78	97
Convenient location	75	77	95
Fast checkout	70	–	–
Personal safety outside store	70	–	–
Good variety, wide selection of brands	–	54	98
Nutrition and health information available for shopper	–	50	84

Source: The State of The Food Marketing Industry, 1995, 1996, 1997. Food Marketing Institute, May 8, May 6, May 5, Chicago, Illinois.

variety or assortment of items available at local retail outlets; purchases can be made online from an unrestricted array of products and from almost any location. Consumers demand more than just a fair price and they get it. Price is an issue, but only one part of today's value equation. Convenience, location, price, quality, and service are **all** part of the consumers' value equation. However, the elements of a specific value equation will vary depending on the consumer group, product or service, and industry.

In this new demassified environment, **consumers rule.** They demand customization and will purchase what they want, when they want it, decide what to pay, and have it delivered according to their preferred form of transportation.

How are companies responding?

PARADIGM SHIFT

Production Era

"[C]onsumers today have to contend with a shopping experience shaped by a distribution infrastructure and marketing strategies that have developed since the 1960s, and that no longer meet the needs of shoppers who have too little time and too much data."

Bruce Westbrook, Deloitte & Touche, *MMR,* Feb. 19, 2001

During World Wars I and II, the United States geared up to manufacture ammunition, guns, tanks, and airplanes. Housewives sacrificed by rationing food, collecting cooking fats, and saving paper and tin. Many women even went to work in the factories. At the end of World War II, men came home to take back manufacturing jobs or go to school. Many got married and had children, creating the "Baby Boomer" generation. The new demand for homes, furnishings, and appliances kept the manufacturing boom going.

Many companies continued to produce defense-related products and technologies throughout the Cold War. Many other companies manufactured products designed to meet the growing consumer demand. The mass market for furniture, housewares, children's clothes and toys, automobiles, radios, and televisions saw continued growth. Economies of scale, chain of command, management control, and efficient production methods were hallmarks of this business paradigm. Prime-time television was an ideal vehicle for reaching this mass market of consumers throughout the nation to demonstrate the newest mass-produced products.

By the 1970s and 1980s, Japan and Germany had rebuilt their factories with state-of-the-art equipment and were successfully selling their products in the United States at competitive prices. This prompted U.S. manufacturers to become more efficient and more price competitive. As a result, quality initiatives and just-in-time manufacturing processes became popular. Many companies still have a production, "build it and they will come" approach to doing business. They may have changed to a small-batch process to fulfill the needs of niche markets and they may have incorporated a quality-control or ISO 9000 process of manufacturing in an effort to reduce costs. They may have gone even further to develop an integrated supply chain approach as a way to further reduce costs. These techniques, however, no longer guarantee success. The mass market is gone. Therefore, creating and selling mass-produced products to a mass consumer market is doomed to failure.

Consumer Era

Toffler's prediction of a demassified society in the United States has come true. In the 1960s and 1970s, network television reached over 90 percent of U.S. households every evening; by 1990 this number was under two-thirds and declining. By the 1997-1998 viewing season, the networks only reached 47 percent of the decreased prime-time viewing audience. The number of magazines catering to specific interests has exploded. *Sports Illustrated* was the only sports magazine at one time; today <www.newsdirectory.com> lists more than 500 different sports magazines.[17] The number of households with VCRs, DVD players, MP3 players, and computers has exploded. The number of people using the Internet continues to rise. Nielsen/Net Ratings reports that 429 million people have Internet access around the world. The result is that there is **no mass consumer group.** There are **no large consumer niches.**

"Mass market is over—the future is about individualization. . . . We have entered a time of one-on-one or customized marketing."

Faith Popcorn, Chairperson, Brain Reserve, *Chain Store Age,* Oct. 1996

Each consumer can seek information from a source of his or her choice and will only buy the products or services that satisfy his or her individual needs. Distribution is no longer a company's decision; the consumer decides how, where, and when he or she wishes to buy and obtain the product or service. You can only sell what a customer wants to buy; you can only sell products in a retail outlet if consumers want to visit that retailer; you can only get the consumers to frequent stores if they enjoy the experience.

"Bargaining power will shift entirely to the consumer, who will search for seamless distribution of their goods and services."

Manly Molpus, CEO, G.M.A. *Food Logistics,* Jan./Feb. 2001

Success in this new consumer era does not come from creating another target segment to whom products can be marketed in a traditional fashion. The consumer-centric approach presented in this book means that the whole organization must be involved in this process. Consumer data must be current and accurate. Inventory and production must be managed from the perspective of consumer consumption. Online, catalog, and in-store sales must be coordinated. This requires major reorganization, coordination of front and back office activities, and use of technology.

A number of recently published books provide insight on this paradigm shift: *One-to-One Marketing* by Peppers and Rogers; *The New Marketing Paradigm* by Schultz, Tannenbaum, and Stanley; *The Customer Century* by Gronstedt; *Customers Rule!* by Blackwell and Stephan; *Grocery Revolution* by Kahn and McAlister; *The Agenda* by Hammer; *Value Space* by Mittal and Sheth; and *The Customer Revolution* by Seybold.

"Winners change the rules of the game by changing the customer's definition of value."

Ralph Stayer, former CEO of Johnsonville Foods, *The Staging Area,* Jan. 1997

Those companies that best identify the nature of shifting consumer groups, individual needs and wants, and consumer use of technology stand the best chance to win, but **ONLY** if the **whole company** is organized around satisfying customer needs.

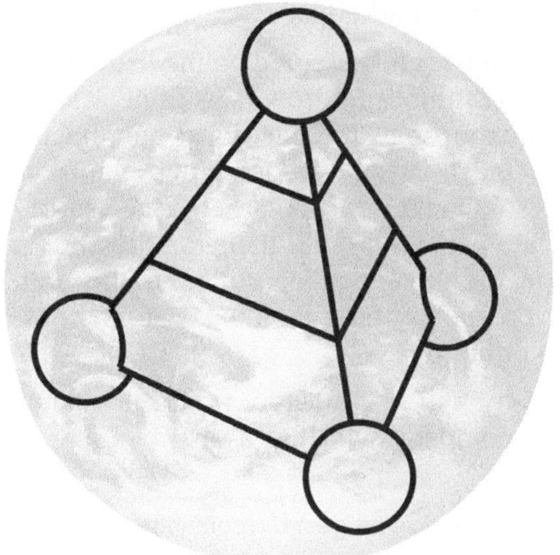

Chapter 3

Global Environment

"You've got to be on the cutting edge of change. You can't simply maintain the status quo, because somebody's always coming from another country with another product, or consumer tastes change, or the cost structure does, or there's a technology breakthrough. If you're not fast and adaptable, you're vulnerable. This is true for every segment of every business in every country in the world."

Jack Welch, CEO, General Electric
Fortune, December 13, 1993

"Eliminating all barriers would boost growth by nearly $2 trillion, which is twice the size of the Chinese economy."

University of Michigan Study, Jan. 23, 2001

Business functions in a global environment. Today, **ALL** business functions in a global environment. Of course, the large global and multinational companies conduct business worldwide. The growth of U.S. exports in recent years has come from small- and medium-sized businesses. By having a Web site on the Internet, many more companies have received inquiries and orders from customers outside their countries.

Even domestic manufacturers and local service companies are involved in the global marketplace.

"In a time of drastic change it is the learners who inherit the future. The learned usually find themselves equipped to live in a world that no longer exists."

Eric Hoffman

The number of countries represented on the list of the 100 largest corporations continues to grow (see Table 3.1). With so many countries exporting products, local manufacturers in most countries find themselves competing against nondomestic products sold in their local markets. Because of immigration, expatriate executives and their families living in the country, and/or foreign students enrolled in universities, even local service companies have a global customer base in their own local communities.

Not every company will manufacture products in another country. Not every company will hire a distributor or sales

TABLE 3.1. World's Largest Corporations

Country	1968	1979	1984	1990	1993	1996	2001
United States	67	47	47	33	32	24	37
Germany	13	13	8	12	14	13	10
Britain	7	7	5	6	4	2	5
France	4	11	5	10	6	13	7
Japan	3	7	12	18	23	29	22
Italy	2	3	3	4	4	4	3
Netherlands/ United Kingdom	2	2	2	2	2	2	2
Switzerland	1	1	2	3	3	5	4
South Korea	–	–	4	2	4	4	1
Mexico	–	1	1	1	1	1	1
Venezuela	–	1	1	1	1	1	1
Netherlands	–	–	–	–	–	–	3
Belgium/ United Kingdom	–	–	–	–	–	–	1
China	–	–	–	–	–	–	3

Source: Adapted from "The World's 500 Largest Industrial Companies," *Fortune,* August 4, 1997, pp. F2-F3; "The World's Largest Corporations," July 23, 2001, <Fortune.com>.

force to sell products outside its domestic market. However, the number of multinational or global companies that are expanding into new markets increases every day. So even though you may not be actively selling to other countries outside your domestic market, you may well be doing business with foreign companies. As a result, owners and managers of even local domestic manufacturing companies must consider the global environment. Therefore, companies must be aware of global competitors and must be ready to adapt to global consumers.

"In the future, I think global will be a matter of integrating strategy structure, standards, and systems across customers, categories, and geography."

Ralph Drayer, Chairman, Supply Chain Insights, *Supermarket News,* June 11, 2001

In 1968 Marshall McLuhan introduced the idea of a global village. Since technology makes worldwide communication easier, since people all over the world receive similar information and entertainment, and since standardized products can be made available globally, many experts suggest that the world may become a single village with one culture, one language, and one set of customer needs. For example, teenagers around the world watch MTV. Specific programs vary in different regions of the world, but many of the songs are the same. The vast majority of children in the developed and developing countries know Mickey Mouse. Children in the United Kingdom, Australia, the United States, or any location that broadcasts British television shows know *Bananas in Pajamas.* Science fiction fans around the world are familiar with both *Star Trek* and *Dr. Who. The Jerry Springer Show* is broadcast all over the United States and the European Union. McDonald's and Coca-Cola seem to be everywhere. Are we moving toward McLuhan's prediction of one global village?

IS STANDARDIZATION INEVITABLE? IT DEPENDS

Maybe we are becoming one village, as McLuhan suggested, but at what level? How deep does it go? Some **consumer products** meeting basic consumer needs may be standardized, such as shampoo, deodorant, diapers, beverages, pens, jeans, detergent, shoes, or cosmetics (see Figure 3.1).

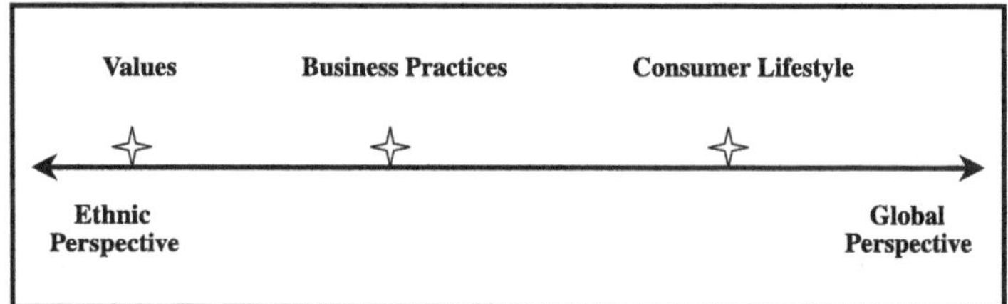

FIGURE 3.1. Movement Toward a "Global Village" Perspective

Pantene, Secret, Huggies, Corona, Bic, Levi's, Ariel, Reebok, or Maybelline are available in the same form around the world. Many consumer products are standardized throughout the world. In terms of **consumer lifestyles** (Figure 3.1), a global perspective may be developing, thereby moving us closer to a global village.

> "The dial tone in Japan sounds like a busy signal to an American. It was pretty confusing to be sitting there in your hotel room thinking you're not getting through when the modem is actually connecting."
>
> Bill Macfarlane, CIO, Smart & Final, *Chain Store Age,* 1999

Business practices, however, are far from standardized; a handshake is not the daily greeting everywhere in the world, one-page memos are not the standard form of communication in all companies, and meetings do not always follow an agenda strictly to the minute.[1] However, there are signs that some business practices are becoming standardized.

For instance, the Japanese formal practice of exchanging business cards has become an important part of business etiquette in many places. In Argentina, a group of business executives were engaged in a lively discussion. People began interrupting one another and one person said, "Wait. We don't do this anymore. One person talks at a time." The explanation offered for this redirection of behavior was that since the introduction of videoconferences with headquarters in the United States, everyone had learned that it was necessary to come to meetings prepared and to let the person speaking finish what was being said before the next person began to speak. Certainly, this approach makes sense when the videoconferencing technology is being used. If two people at different locations speak, no one can hear what is being said. However, this practice was now being adopted in this subsidiary in Argentina for face-to-face meetings in Argentina.

Some business practices are becoming standardized, but many are not changing. The importance of social activities in Latin America or the significance of personal relationships in Asia have not changed. Other business practices are not standardized and can create difficult situations. For instance, activities that can be classified as bribery are not viewed the same way around the world (see Table 3.2). Some countries have strict standards, laws, or norms against forms of brib-

TABLE 3.2. Top Twenty-Five and Bottom Twenty-Five Countries on the 2001 Corruption Perception Index (CPI)*

Top 25			Bottom 25		
Country	**Rank**	**CPI Score**	**Country**	**Rank**	**CPI Score**
Finland	1	9.9	Costa Rica	40	4.5
Denmark	2	9.5	Mauritius	40	4.5
New Zealand	3	9.4	Greece	42	4.2
Iceland	4	9.2	South Korea	42	4.2
Singapore	4	9.2	Peru	44	4.1
Sweden	6	9.0	Poland	44	4.1
Canada	7	8.9	Brazil	46	4.0
Netherlands	8	8.8	Bulgaria	47	3.9
Luxembourg	9	8.7	Croatia	47	3.9
Norway	10	8.6	Czech Republic	47	3.9
Australia	11	8.5	Colombia	50	3.8
Switzerland	12	8.4	Mexico	51	3.7
United Kingdom	13	8.3	Panama	51	3.7
Hong Kong	14	7.9	Slovak Republic	51	3.7
Austria	15	7.8	Egypt	54	3.6
Israel	16	7.6	El Salvador	54	3.6
United States	16	7.6	Turkey	54	3.6
Chile	18	7.5	Argentina	57	3.5
Ireland	18	7.5	China	57	3.5
Germany	20	7.4	Ghana	59	3.4
Japan	21	7.1	Latvia	59	3.4
Spain	22	7.0	Malawi	61	3.2
France	23	6.7	Thailand	61	3.2
Belgium	24	6.6	Dominican Republic	63	3.1
Portugal	25	6.3	Moldova	63	3.1

Source: Adapted from "2001 Corruption Perceptions Index," Internet Center for Corruption Research, Transparency International. Available at <www.globaledge.msu.edu>.

*2000 CPI Score related to perceptions of the degree of corruption as seen by businesspeople, risk analysts, and the general public and ranges between 10 (highly clean) and 0 (highly corrupt).

ery; other countries view forms of bribery as accepted business practices. Certainly, not all business practices are standardized. Business practices are not as far along the ethnic-global continuum in Figure 3.1 as consumer products.

> "Ironically, as the legal and bureaucratic barriers to international trade fall, cultural and linguistic barriers continue to rise."
>
> Anna Radzievsky, *Trade and Culture,* 1996

Values are becoming standardized at a glacial pace. Psychologists say that people's values are formed by the time they are about twelve years of age. Attitudes and beliefs toward human rights, control of nature, relationships, and ethics vary considerably around the world.

Some religions believe in universal truths that are immutable; some philosophies believe in doing what is necessary to preserve harmony. Some religions believe that human beings have a soul so they are different from other living things. Some religions believe that all living things have a soul so humans are not different from plants or animals.

Some cultures believe that successfully completing tasks in the allotted amount of time is the measure of being professional. Some cultures believe in an unstable world, and, therefore, security comes from family or close-knit networks. As a result, spending time building and maintaining family or network relationships is more important than completing tasks within an allotted amount of time.

While each generation has values that are different from the previous generation, the overall values of a country change very slowly. Changing values between generations do not necessarily result in a worldwide convergence of values. Furthermore, different values result in distinctly different business decisions. In those countries with a high value on family relationships, nepotism is a highly valued criterion when hiring employees or choosing companies with which to do business. Nepotism is illegal in those countries emphasizing tasks, systems, and objectivity over family relationships. Values are still distinctly different among cultural groups, reflecting an ethnic perspective and resulting in significantly different business behaviors around the world.

Consumers in geographically distant locations may purchase some of the same products, some business practices may be converging, but business decision making will not converge as long as basic values differ from culture to culture. **The global village doesn't exist yet.**

ADAPTATION

How should businesses approach this global marketplace? It depends. Are you selling products to other countries? Which countries have large markets (see Table 3.3)? Do your products fit the needs of consumers in those countries with large markets? Are you manufacturing in another country? Do you need to manage employees in another country? Are you working with distributors or joint venture partners? How risky it is to do business in another country (see Table 3.4)? The concept of adaptation implies that different decisions will be made in three kinds of business circumstances: selling to local consumers, managing employees, and working with strategic partners.

TABLE 3.3. World's Largest Countries in 2001

Country	Population (Millions)
China	1,273
India	1,033
United States	285
Indonesia	206
Brazil	172
Pakistan	145
Russia	144
Bangladesh	134
Japan	127
Nigeria	127
Mexico	100
Germany	82
Vietnam	79
Philippines	77
Egypt	70

Source: Population Reference Bureau, May 2001, ISSN 0085-8315.

TABLE 3.4. Ten Most Risky and Ten Least Risky Countries

Ten Least Risky	Ten Most Risky
Singapore	Sierra Leone
Norway	Yugoslavia
Switzerland	Somalia
Luxembourg	Guinea-Bissau
Netherlands	Zimbabwe
Finland	Congo, Democratic Republic
Brunei	Iraq
Denmark	Moldova
Canada	Korea, Democratic People's Republic
Sweden	Liberia

Source: International Country Risk Guide, The PRS Group, Inc., <www.prsgroup.com>, 1999-2000.

"In Scandinavia the living room is furnished for conversation, so sofas are sturdy hard-cushioned and straight backed. In America, where the television dominates the living room, sofas need to be softer and fluffier."

Steen Kanter, Kanter International, *Chain Store Age,* 1999

Consumers may have similar needs, such as washing clothes, preparing food, or purchasing machinery for manufacturing. However, identical products do not always sell well around the world. Most countries in the world use the metric system so U.S. products need to be calibrated and/or labeled in metric terms when sold in other countries. The voltage and frequency available in outlets are not the same around the world so electric products need to be modified to work in local conditions. Video systems use different standards around the world so videotapes recorded on a particular system are not compatible worldwide.

Washing machines are considered to be necessities in developed countries, but in the People's Republic of China they are status symbols. Owning a washing machine is so important that it is put on display in front of the house. Since the supply of electricity is unstable and expensive, the washing machine may not be used often, if at all.

Some similarities may exist within a region or across specific regions. Ralston Purina conducted a worldwide study of pet care by asking 6,200 dog-owning households and 6,300 cat-owning households in seven countries (United States, Germany, Brazil, Mexico, Spain, Italy, and Argentina) to complete a questionnaire. Results revealed seven distinct groups of pet owners that were similar across these countries.[2] Based upon their mission and objectives, Ralston Purina could identify the segments of most interest to them, could create targeted merchandising strategies, and make decisions about the appropriate assortment for specific stores.

Taste is one area in which differences do exist. The amount and kinds of spices used vary from one ethnic group to another. For instance, the amount of sugar used to sweeten chocolate varies—Europeans prefer dark chocolate while U.S. consumers prefer milk chocolate. Nestle's instant coffee sold in Spain is different from the coffee sold in the United Kingdom, which is different from the coffee sold in Sweden.

> "Too many retailers don't pay attention to differences of doing business in different countries."
>
> Rolando de Aguiar
> CFO, Ames Dept. Store, 1999

McDonald's sells American culture as well as food around the world. McDonald's does not adapt its trademark foods. Hamburgers and french fries served at any McDonald's around the world taste the same as or much like those served in the United States as possible. However, McDonald's adapts to the taste and preferences of local consumers in other ways. For example, McDonald's adapts its menu by creating food items that appeal to local tastes, such as fried rice in Japan and vegetarian burgers in India. However, whether consumers are eating "American" hamburgers or fried rice at McDonald's, they are also sampling American culture.

Hollywood movie studios found that there is a limit to the appeal of American pop culture. While major Hollywood movies are a huge draw worldwide and while English may be the language of the international blockbuster, some lower-budget movies, in almost any language, such as Roberto Benigni's *Life Is Beautiful,* can become blockbuster hits. In addition, most audiences prefer local TV shows.[3] Success in this industry is knowing when, where, and how to adapt to local preferences.

Wal-Mart has certainly had a difficult time trying to reapply their best practices around the world. Wal-Mart's first international expansion outside the United States was into Mexico. On the one hand, Wal-Mart did not share its technological know-how and global buying power with its new partner, Cifra, and carried many items that Mexicans rarely used, such as ice skates, riding lawn mowers, fishing equipment, and clay pigeons for skeet shooting. As a result, inventory quickly got away from Wal-Mart. A similar problem occurred in Argentina when Wal-Mart did not take time to learn about the local marketplace and tried to sell hardware appliances that were incompatible with the voltage in the local power grid.[4] Having a computerized system that is extremely efficient in one market does not mean it will be equally successful everywhere. Products that sell well in one market do not necessarily sell well in other markets. The computerized inventory system has had to be modified for local requirements and the assortment of products has had to be changed to meet consumer needs.

If consumer needs are the same everywhere or if your product represents your country's culture and that is what you are trying to sell, then products can be standardized. If, however, consumer needs differ, structural differences exist, or consumer tastes or preferences differ, products and services need to be adapted for a specific market.

"Jobs supported by international trade pay up to 13-18% more than the national average."

International Trade Administration, U.S. Department of Commerce, April 2001

Employees use different business practices in many cases. In countries with poor distribution systems, money may not motivate employees to increase productivity because there are few products in the stores to purchase. Some companies need to adapt to religious differences not just by identifying the correct holidays but by allowing employees the opportunity to stop work and pray at specific times during the day.

Empowerment is not a universally accepted principle. In countries that value equality, empowerment is a business approach that allows decision making to take place at lower levels in the organization with employees taking responsibility for decisions they make. In other countries that value status and hierarchy, decision making is centralized and employees are expected to follow orders. Volunteering to make decisions is not desirable business behavior. In those areas of the world in which people believe in fate, one cannot presume to know the future or to control the future. Therefore, employees will not volunteer to make individual decisions or take responsibility for decisions.

In one company in Latin America the employees came in every morning and spent about an hour chatting with one another about what they had done the night before, what they had eaten or where they had gone for dinner, and the well-being of their families before getting down to work. The manager was from the United States and frustrated about all the time being wasted so he called a meeting and told everyone to limit their personal conversations to five minutes in the morning or have one hour's worth of pay deducted from their paychecks. The employees did as directed and productivity fell considerably below what it had been. The atmosphere became tense and morale was low. With no improvement over time, the manager withdrew the directive of only five minutes of conversation in the morning. The employees went back to talking for an hour and productivity not only went back to earlier levels but exceeded them. In Latin America, connecting with families and close friends is important. As a result, spending time in the morning talking with co-workers and reconnecting was essential for setting a good tone for working before devoting time to tasks. On the other hand, in some countries co-workers do not spend time in personal conversation at the beginning of the day and may not even use one another's first names even if they have worked together for several years.

Relationships between managers and employees are not the same around the world. If you are managing a sales force, supervising employees in a manufacturing facility, or providing services, understanding the local assumptions about how employees work is critical for success.

Strategic alliances or partnerships are being used more often as companies combine complementary products, share areas of expertise, or cooperate on research activities. Many of these partnerships, mergers, or strategic alliances involve companies from different countries. For instance Harte Hanks, a U.S. based direct marketing company, created a strategic alliance with WPP Group, a Singaporean direct mail company. WPP had an established group of customers and good creative talent who successfully designed and wrote outstanding direct mail pieces for Southeast Asia. Harte Hanks, on the other hand, wanted to expand into Southeast Asia but had no particular expertise in that area of the world. They did, however, have excellent software that could track fulfillment and measure the results of direct marketing activities. In this case, the alliance made sense because each partner had an area of expertise that the other partner did not.

The most common reason given for the failure of alliances is culture clash—even if the companies are from the same country. While the alliance may make sense financially, in terms of market coverage, from a product innovation perspective, or from a cost-efficiency perspective, the alliance will fail if the cultural differences are not managed. For example, two companies in the security industry decided to merge because each company had expertise in different kinds of security. After the merger, the umbrella company offered a broader range of services to clients. During the merger negotiations the president of one company clearly wanted to be president and take charge of the merged company. To help balance control, both companies maintained their headquarters and divided functions, such that each headquarters housed part of the top management group. While this arrangement appeared to satisfy all the requirements and issues of control, over time the two organizations did not see the merged company going in the same direction. Ultimately, the merged company split up into the two original companies.

"Although improving efficiency, joint ventures have also created problems because of different goals, values, and cultures."

Michael Y. Hy and Haiyang Chen, *Journal of Business Research,* Feb. 1966

One of the most successful joint ventures in the United States is CFM—a joint venture between GE Aircraft Engines and SNECMA, a manufacturer of airplane engines in France. For any airplane engine project secured by the joint venture, the tasks of building the engine are split as equally as possible between the two companies. The companies do not share costs, only revenue. Each company performs its part of the project within the designated deadline; each company receives 49 percent of the revenue (2 percent of the revenue is used to maintain the headquarters of the joint venture which has a staff of about ten people). Each partner is motivated to keep costs as low as possible because their profit is the difference between their costs and the revenue received. Each partner may make a different amount of profit depending upon their cost structure. This arrangement does not eliminate all conflict by any means. However, agreeing upon the projects to be pursued, designating clear areas of responsibility, and determining how revenue will be allocated ahead of time goes a long way toward establishing the structure for a successful venture.

If business practices are different, if decision-making processes are different, if the goals of the organization are different, if the values of the companies are different, continued frustration, tension, and failed initiatives will take their toll.

Business takes place in a global marketplace. Every company must decide what position it will take in this global environment.

- Companies that choose to remain domestic need to evaluate their current and potential customer base: How many current or potential customers are from another country and, of that group, how many need special products or services?
- Companies that choose to remain domestic must constantly be aware of global competitors bringing new products to the local market.
- Companies selling products in other countries must make a decision about standardization: Are you selling your country's culture? Does your product fit customers' needs that are universal or do differences among customers demand adaptation?
- Have you learned enough about the culture and business practices in a particular country to be able to effectively evaluate potential distributors or employees?
- Have you learned enough about the country in which you have established a retail outlet or manufacturing facility to effectively manage the employees?
- Have you taken the time to determine the objectives, values, and culture of the company with which you plan to merge?
- All business exists in a global marketplace.

Determine your position. Make sure you know your current customers well. Do your homework regarding competitors: domestic and global. Evaluate potential partners well and take time to reconcile cultural differences. Remembering that you operate in a global environment, maintaining flexibility, and keeping your focus on consumer needs are critical for success. Remember that consumers around the world seek the same thing . . . **VALUE!**

Consumers demand that products and services meet their specific needs. Companies strive to identify needs that apply across global markets. Consumers search for products and services that are customized to meet individual needs. Determining when and what kind of customization is necessary, desirable, and profitable for which products in which markets is critical for success in today's global marketplace. Constantly monitoring the balance required for success in a rapidly changing marketplace is the key for continued success. What does **VALUE** mean to your current consumers in today's marketplace and is that different from yesterday's definition of value? Can you answer the critical question, **"Where do I add value?"**

Section II: Elements of the Consumer-Centric Business Paradigm

"The mix of power is shifting to the consumer in a quiet but powerful manner. . . . The development of 'Consumer Partnership' requires three-way partnership between retailer, supplier and consumer."

Peter Lynch
"Developing Consumer Partnership"
Partnering Group, November 1999

As this shift in power takes place, what are the business process changes required? First, all the players need to focus on the consumer and develop clear consumer insight. Second, collaboration among suppliers, intermediaries, and retailers is necessary for long-term success.

The three chapters in this section look at building a consumer-centric business from each of the industry perspectives: supplier, distributor, and intermediary. Technology is available to facilitate any business practice, process, or procedure. Choosing and deploying technology is **NOT** a program, **NOT** a project, **NOT** a system, **NOT** just technology, and **NOT** just another expense reduction. It **IS** a business process change.

Collaboration among all these players in the supply and demand chain is critical for success and means that the traditional linear supply chain orientation is not the path for success. Section II examines the players (suppliers, intermediaries, and retailers) independently and interdependently. Section III will focus on technology and business processes.

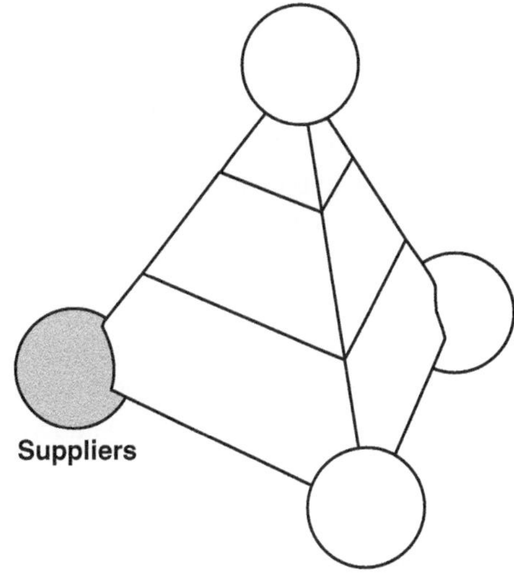

Chapter 4

Suppliers (Suppliers, Producers, Manufacturers)

"[F]or all practical purposes, the mass market is dead."

Ryan Matthews, Futurist
First Matter, LLC

"Traditional supply-chain management focus must give way to demand chain management. It's pretty simple. Buy what your customers buy—and make sure it is available when the customer wants it."

Ken Fobes, Chairman, Strategy Partners Group, *Executive Technology,* May 2000

The demassified, fragmented global market of multidimensional consumers poses a new challenge for manufacturers who think in terms of economies of scale production. During the 1990s companies began to incorporate small batch, flexible manufacturing techniques as they adopted just-in-time philosophies. In the mid-1990s the grocery and consumer packaged goods (CPG) industries reorganized the supply chain. Suppliers wanted full access to information about targeted consumers so they could introduce products that competed on true market value and find effective methods for introducing new products.[1] As a result, they developed processes and models that base manufacturing decisions on what consumers actually buy, thereby instituting a "pull" replenishment system based on consumption.

"Consumer-Driven Innovation Is Our Lifeblood."

Procter & Gamble Co.
MMR, Feb. 11, 2002

New products have been introduced into the marketplace at an ever-increasing rate. In the mid-1990s about 20,000 new products were introduced annually into the grocery and CPG industry. By the year 2000 more than 30,000 new products were introduced to the marketplace.[2] Many of these new products are line extensions or expansions rather than new-to-the-world products. New product introductions are expensive, each one typically costing between $15 million and $20 million. This is an even more expensive proposition when 80 to 90 percent of new products do not last more than eighteen months. In this confusing marketplace, consumers have become less loyal today than they were ten years ago and switch products more often.

"True breakthrough comes from maintaining a paradoxical view that allows one to pursue two seemingly contradictory objectives."

Built to Last

Determining what to produce, in what quantity, for what time period, and at what price is a complex decision. Balancing the competing demands of the marketplace is a challenge. How do you choose new products that will be successful in the marketplace? How do you balance customization of products with profitability? How do you ensure being in-stock for the consumer while optimizing inventories throughout the supply chain? How do you decide which of the current products should be eliminated when introducing new products so that the overall assortment of products offered by your company does not skyrocket out of control? What's the difference among customer satisfaction, loyalty, and retention? The ability to balance competing demands is critical for success.

Where do you begin? Companies need to make four decisions:

1. Develop a clearly articulated mission and strategy.
2. Adopt collaborative business processes.
3. Obtain knowledge about consumers and the marketplace.
4. Decide which tools are needed to accomplish your mission.

MISSION AND STRATEGY

If you don't know where you are going, any decision can be justified. In the great fairy tale of *Alice in Wonderland,* Alice comes to a fork in the road and asks the Cheshire cat, "Which road do I take?" His response is a question: "Where do you want to go?" "I don't know," Alice answers. "Then," says the cat, "it really doesn't matter."

The number of tools available, such as new software programs touted by management gurus, industry seminars, and advertising, are increasing exponentially. The one that is right for your company is the one that fits your mission and strategies. Adopting a tool just because it worked for another company or because the industry is promoting it will **NOT** necessarily make your company successful.

A new tool or technique is useful to your company **ONLY** if it moves your company forward toward achieving the goals derived from your mission and strategy. A tool or technique used in isolation does not generate success. A tool or technique tied specifically to your mission and strategy enables your company to move forward on the continuous journey of implementing the company's mission.

So the first stop is knowing what your company stands for, what it wants to be known for, or what position it wants to occupy in the consumer's mind.

"[M]ethods of simplification and consolidation on the supply side of the value chain will have to be complemented by methods of differentiation on the demand side."

"Customers Value Management," Summary Report, PriceWaterhouse-Coopers, 1999

COLLABORATION

Collaborative business processes are essential if a manufacturer plans to be part of an efficient supply chain basing replenishment decisions on consumer purchases. Small batch production and customizing products for the mass market require collaboration with other business organizations and consumers to determine what quantity of which products should be manufactured when and at what price. The success of suppliers, intermediaries, and retailers depends upon collaborative business processes. The techniques and tools of collaboration will be discussed in more detail in the Business Processes section of the book. In today's environment, it is important to recognize the need for strategic alliances and the need to work interdependently.

CONSUMER AND MARKETPLACE KNOWLEDGE

"The first step is to know who your end customers—and your prospective customers—are and then to learn as much about them as possible."

Patricia Seybold, customers.com, 1998

No decisions can be made without accurate, timely information about consumers and the marketplace. All companies need to focus on end consumers. No matter where you are in the supply chain, timely and accurate consumption information is critical for manufacturing decisions aimed at reliable replenishment. Scanning data are critical for knowing what consumers purchase. No matter how far removed your company may be from end consumer purchases, that information is still essential for accurate manufacturing decisions.

That information, however, does not explain how or why consumers buy. To make decisions that balance seemingly paradoxical goals, companies also need to know what is taking place in the marketplace:

- What types of innovations are being tested?
- What consumer products or services are now feasible because of new research?
- Which business processes are being used successfully by competitors or by companies in other industries?
- What new technologies could benefit your company?

Each company determines its own mission and strategy that provides a unique view of the marketplace, determining what the company stands for and what relationship it has to each of its constituent groups (shareholders, consumers, employees, suppliers, and the community). Collaborative business processes will be examined in the next section of the book. This chapter will concentrate on the topics of Consumer Knowledge and Marketplace Innovation.

Customer Knowledge

As a manufacturer, do you know why the end consumers purchase your product or service, what their preferences are, what type of individual adaptation they would prefer, or what specific needs your product or service satisfies? Can you identify where and how you add **VALUE** for the consumer? Unless you can answer these questions, how can you design products and services that consumers will purchase, use, and want to purchase again? If you cannot answer these questions, your consumers are easy targets for companies with innovative products and services that better meet their needs.

Traditionally, survey research has been used to identify similarities among consumers, thereby allowing a company to identify target segments. These target segments would be marketed to, advertised to, and communicated with using the same tools. However, a target market of "similar" consumers does **NOT** provide good enough knowledge anymore.

"The Customer Satisfaction Index is down, with consumers voicing rising dissatisfaction with companies."

The Wall Street Journal, May 21, 2001

As the "Baby Boomer" generation ages and becomes more conscious of specific health problems, their needs are changing.[3] Datamonitor, a U.K. consumer research company, predicts a decreased demand for vitamin supplements and an increased demand for foods containing ingredients that target specific ailments. For example, Benecol spread claims to help **reduce** cholesterol levels and Yakult, a fermented milk drink, claims to maintain a favorable balance of bacteria in the digestive system.

In 1999, the Federal Drug Administration claimed that soy might reduce the risk of heart disease, but Americans have been reluctant to adopt traditional soy foods like tofu or soy milk.[4] Soy flour is being incorporated into bread in countries outside the United States. The Ohio State University is negotiating to license a soy bread recipe to bakeries that would put soy bread on the grocery shelves, in school lunches, and in sub shops. Individuals now have access to more information, more suppliers, and more products or services than just the ones your company provides or the ones available in a local geography. About 204 nutraceutical-type products have been introduced into the world's biggest markets in the last two years. If another product or service fits a consumer's individual needs more specifically, he or she will abandon your product or service.

Whether the products are airplanes, automobiles, or consumer products, suppliers must respond to the paradoxical demands of customization and cost reduction.[5] While survival may depend upon cost reduction, growth depends upon product development with increasing customization. Consumers, suppliers, and intermediaries need to be involved throughout the product development process so the consumers get what they want, when they want it, and for a price they are willing to pay. The suppliers' challenge is to customize products or services while keeping costs in line.

Examples

For instance, the **National Industrial Bicycle Company of Japan** (NIBCJ) takes the measurements of each customer as well as information about riding style, frequency, and locations where the consumer prefers riding. Based on this information, NIBCJ designs a bicycle customizing tire tread, handlebar, seat, wheels, brakes, gears, and even the paint color.[6] As a consumer, would you rather go to a sporting goods store and select a bike based upon the manufacturer's assessment of what a "typical" mountain biker wants OR would you rather spend forty-five minutes answering questions and get a bicycle that fits your specifications exactly? Where would you go next time you were in the market for a bicycle: to the sporting goods store with choices designed for a "typical" target segment, to another company that makes individualized bicycles to answer questions all over again, **OR** to the company that already has your measurements and successfully designed a bike for you last time? If the company did a good job creating the individualized product AND providing individualized service, you will find it much easier to return to the company that already has your information on file. Individualizing products and services is one way of developing a strong relationship with the consumer.

Balancing individualization and profitability in an effort to meet consumer needs is a critical issue. Not every consumer needs a customized bicycle or is willing to pay for one. How important having the latest technology is, or whether cycling is a serious athletic activity, a means of earning a living, or an important hobby, not only determines whether a consumer desires customization, but also whether the consumer is willing to pay a higher price for it.

Dell Computer offers customers two choices: limited customization or specific customization. Consumers are offered a range of standard alternative choices from which they can pick and configure a computer that will be delivered within a reasonably short period of time (a few days to a couple of weeks depending upon the availability of parts, speed of payment authorization, and type of delivery service chosen by the consumer). Consumers who want to design a computer beyond the range of choices routinely offered also have that opportunity. Consumers can request computers built to their exact specifications. Delivery, however, will take a longer time. Parts may not be as readily available, assembly may take longer, and configuration may take longer. If consumers are willing to wait, they can have a computer designed to their exact specifications. In both cases, price depends upon the components selected. The prices are provided to consumers so they can make trade-offs between components and price while designing a machine within their desired price range to meet their specifications.

Food companies are responding to the needs of consumers for convenience and customized meal solutions. **Del Monte** is selling fruit in jars that are resealable. **Campbell's** not only sells soup in traditional condensed form in cans and Chunky soup in cans but also sells soups in pop-top cans and resealable jars. Ready-to-serve entrees are appearing from a variety of manufacturers.[7] **General Mills** is preparing to provide consumers with the opportunity to create and name their own cereal.[8] Consumers will be able to select from more than 100 different ingredients to create their own breakfast cereal and then give it a name. The cereal will then be delivered to the consumers' homes in a one or two week supply of single-serving portions.

Consumers' expectations are being raised by companies that do provide opportunities for individualizing products and services. Direct feedback from consumers using your product or service is important. If your company does not meet consumers' needs, another company will. A combination of data sources is necessary, usually requiring collaboration with other companies. **Understanding consumers is critical for success.**

Consumer Feedback

The first step in this orientation of getting more direct input from consumers was the introduction of 1-800 phone numbers. Consumers could call companies with questions, suggestions, complaints, or orders. Creating two-way communication with consumers has been so successful in the United States, that the phone companies have had to add 1-888 and 1-877 prefixes because of demand. Automatic call centers for outbound calls to potential consumers or for inbound calls receiving orders, questions, or complaints exploded in popularity, creating the field of telephony (combining computers and telephone technology).

Customer service representatives (CSRs) can talk with any consumer from any location. CSRs can answer calls for more than one company as long as the name of the company being called by the consumer flashes on the computer screen as the CSRs answer the phone. With a few pieces of identifying information, CSRs can answer questions about the consumer's account or take orders over the phone. Because phone lines can direct calls to any location, the call center does not have to be at headquarters and may even be outsourced to an independent company. An independent company may represent several organizations—as long as the computer downloads the appropriate information to the computer screen of the person answering the call.

In fact, the call center can be anywhere. For example, the offices of Customer Assets appear to be located in Santa Fe, New Mexico, with frosted glass and funky amber lights playing off turquoise walls. One of the employees answers the phone saying, "Hi, my name is Susan Sanders." Her fluent English and broad vowel sounds certainly place her in the Midwest. A visitor's sense of disorientation watching "Susan" answer questions about her personal life (e.g., getting her degree at the University of Illinois) or hearing American slang phrases such as "No way, José" only becomes stronger when leaving the office and entering the streets of Bangalore.[9] This call center is in India. Employees watch a lot of contemporary U.S. television shows (e.g., *Friends*) to learn current idiomatic phrases, create a fictional background to use when answering personal questions, and use "all-American" idioms when at work. As long as the company CSRs can respond to consumers' questions with problem-solving advice and develop rapport with consumers, the call center's physical location can be anywhere. There may even be more than one call center located in physically distant locations taking advantage of time differences and enabling the company to provide service twenty-four hours a day, seven days a week (24/7).

Data collected from the call centers, however, need to be managed. Knowing which customers ordered which items, in what amounts, how often, and with what method of payment enables companies to determine which consumers are most valuable. Customer Relationship Management (CRM) software has been available since 1985. Initially, it focused on lead generation and contact management.[10] Mining the data to determine when consumers purchase, how often, how much, and how they react to price changes can direct where and how manufacturers spend marketing dollars. For instance, Kraft executives used this kind of data to direct a different mix of marketing elements to specific target segments, such as the 100 percent brand loyal group. As a result of this adaptation of marketing tactics, Kraft increased annual sales by 21 percent and gross margin by 9 percent.[11] The General Mills Web site that allows consumers to create customized

"Instead of expecting the customer to use information to make a purchase, the 1:1 enterprise uses information about individual customers to figure out what each one needs next."

Don Peppers and Martha Rogers, PhD, *Marketing Tools*, 1998

cereals will create databases that not only collect consumer purchase history data but also make health and nutritional databases available as resources for consumers when they are creating their cereals.

As the telephony field becomes more sophisticated, so does CRM software. Companies can assign consumers to specific CSRs; when the phone rings the computer identifies the phone number and directs the call to the designated CSR, so that by the time the phone is answered the computer screen displays the consumer's account information (i.e., company, past orders, costs, payment terms). The CSR can then personalize a greeting and respond to specific questions regarding the consumer's account, current purchases, or past purchases. CSRs have a specific group of consumers with whom they interact repeatedly over time, thereby building strong consumer relationships.

One-on-one relationships are critical to good consumer care. Examining what consumers purchase in what combinations or, maybe even more importantly, what consumers purchase separately can provide opportunities. For instance, if you know that 60 percent of consumers purchase baby wipes but not diapers or that 50 percent of consumers purchasing razors do not purchase shaving cream or that 41 percent of consumers buy toothpaste but not toothbrushes, you can identify opportunities to create consumer solutions by serving their needs better and adding value to their transactions with your company.[12]

"It is now possible to engage individual customers based on their unique preferences."

"Marketing to Segments of One: Tips," www.ideabeat.com, March 3, 2001

As companies incorporate Internet applications, CRM software capabilities continue to expand. The Internet provides another capability for two-way communication with end consumers. If the company provides contact information on its Web site, consumers can ask questions, voice concerns, request new product adaptations or services, or participate in product development processes. By providing Frequently Asked Questions and Answers, consumers can find answers and solve problems when they arise, at any time of the day or night.

If chat rooms are available, consumers can talk with one another about problems faced, alternatives tried, continuing frustrations, or best solutions, developing a sense of community among consumer groups. Kimberly-Clark has found the Internet to be useful for getting consumer feedback about personal issues such as bed-wetting, menstruation, and adult incontinence. Either the camaraderie of chatting with others who have a similar problem or asking for information or suggestions from an anonymous source reduces the amount of embarrassment a consumer feels.[13] These conversations have provided the company with useful information for product adaptations or line extensions. Some companies have even set up special Web sites used by selected consumers to respond to new ideas, new products, or new services.

Interactivity is critical for learning what consumers are thinking, why they have the preferences they do, and what provokes negative reactions. Today's CRM software is able to capture that information and incorporate it with consumer purchases so that, not only is consumer loyalty and retention fostered, but also lifetime metrics of consumers can be tracked to determine consumer value. Then, companies can make consumer care decisions and maintain profitability. However, gathering information about current or potential consumers is not successful if it is the **ONLY** source of information.

"As the ground lurches beneath them, companies more than ever must look ahead and be ready to leap to new terrain."

Amy Cortese, *BusinessWeekOnline,* March 23, 2001

Innovation in the Marketplace

Consumers like innovations and have an interest in trying new products. However, with 20,000 to 30,000 CPG products being introduced to the marketplace each year consumers are often confused by the array of choices before them. With seventy-two varieties of Pantene, the selection of shampoo and styling gels has grown so confusing that packaging has been changed to be more descriptive of results (e.g., "volume" or "smooth, sleek and straight" instead of hair types such as "normal" or "oily") and Procter & Gamble supplies pamphlets explaining Pantene's styling tonic, mousse, and gel.[14]

"Meaningful additions in the right categories, skillfully aimed at appreciative target consumers can be a key to lengthening margins, increasing register ring and creating consumer value and loyalty."

Efficient Assortment: The Process and the Benefits, ECR Publication, 1996

Does this assortment provide consumers with choices they want or does it generate confusion?

Collaboratively, Procter & Gamble and Kroger conducted a study in 1994-1995 with laundry detergent to determine consumers' responses to a decreased assortment of product (see Table 4.1). After examining the number of SKUs and tracking historical sales, Kroger and Procter & Gamble decreased the number of SKUs on the shelf by 13 percent or 29 percent, depending upon the division. Both Procter & Gamble's sales volume increased and Kroger's market share in laundry detergent increased. Consumers indicated that they thought more items were on the shelf. In reality, there were fewer SKUs, but more of the items the consumers wanted to purchase were on the shelf when the consumer wanted them.

Too great a number of items with small differences is confusing to consumers. Unilever is currently working to decrease its portfolio of brands from 1,600 to 970 or fewer. Determining the appropriate assortment of items is critical but must be done collaboratively by suppliers and retailers sharing data and consumer insights.

Consumers do appear to be interested in and receptive to new products. Colgate-Palmolive found that 38 percent of their sales came from products introduced within the past five years and that 61 percent of U.S. sales came from recent product introductions.[15] Manufacturers need to be aware of

TABLE 4.1. Efficient Assortment Pilot Study, Laundry—P&G and Kroger

Kroger Divisions	Old SKUs	New SKUs	% Change	P&G Volume (%)	Kroger Market Share (%)
Louisville (8/94)	106	92	–13	+15	+5
Central (11/94)	106	94	–13	+7	+4
Dallas (2/95)	132	103	–29	+10	+8

Source: Trucksis, Brad and Alan Tomlin (1997), Presentation to All Food Group from Japan at Xavier University.

innovations in the marketplace and be ready to take advantage of them.

Manufacturers need to be aware of new ideas, technologies, or processes. Real innovation must encompass a "new mode of thought, a change in business processes, or even a rift in the structure of the organization"[16] that could fundamentally change products, services, or processes. Often these fundamental changes are not immediately accepted. Consider the following:

- "Everything that can be invented has been invented." (Charles Duell, U.S. Patent Office, 1899)
- "The radio craze will die out soon." (Thomas Edison, 1922)
- "Drill for oil . . . are you crazy? You mean drill into the ground to try to find oil?" (Edwin Drake, 1859)
- "TV won't last because people will soon tire of staring at a plywood box every night." (Darryl Zannuck, 20th Century Fox, 1946)
- "There is a world market for about 5 computers." (Tom Watson, Chairman of IBM, 1943)

"We're talking about product life cycles of two to three years or even less. We're talking industry life cycles of less than a decade."

Tapan Munroe, University of San Francisco, *Time,* Oct. 4, 1999

New technologies always seem far-fetched. The ones with major impact fulfill specific consumer needs. Napster shook up the music world by making it possible for consumers to select songs of their own choosing and create a CD specifically designed for them, something they had never been able to do before. Using Napster, consumers could create customized CDs rather than purchasing a CD with a collection of songs the music company thought would appeal to members of the target market.

A new field called nanotechnology involves creating computers at an atomic level, making it possible to weave hybrid machines into many everyday activities. For instance, nanotechnology in athletic T-shirts would enable the shirt to monitor heart rate, keep track of body temperature and respiration, and count calories being burned during exercise sessions. Clothing may be able to "talk" to washing machines with instructions for how it should be washed. You may be able to keep track of children with global positioning systems (GPS) in the collars of their jackets.[17] Using a new metal alloy, "smart shirts" would automatically roll up both sleeves when it is too hot. These shirts never need ironing because the new metal returns to its original shape with the heat of a hair dryer. These shirts are available for $3,750.[18]

The research at Palo Alto Research Center laid the foundation for the mouse, graphical user interface (desktop icon), laser printer, and ethernet. Even though Xerox funded the basic research for these products, the company did not create final products that profited from this research. Companies need the expertise not only to do the basic research but also to recognize **applicable** breakthrough findings that will provide **value** to consumers and to make those products profitably.

"Innovation has moved from a good idea to an imperative."

Paul Saffo, Director, Institute for the Future, *BusinessWeek Online,* March 23, 2001

"Yet it is a rare company that is willing to change course, to cut loose its own successful products so that it can develop something more radical."

Clayton Christansen, *The Innovator's Dilemma*

Innovation does not always involve technology and new products; it can also involve restructuring an organization, changing manufacturing processes, or adding services. Sometimes these radical measures are necessary to stay on course toward fulfilling a company's mission. For example, PepsiCo has a focus on nonalcoholic drinks and snacks. In an effort to continue movement in this direction, Pepsi purchased Tropicana and then Quaker Oats (owner of Gatorade).[19]

Jack Welch identified services as an important direction for the future, sold off product lines, purchased CBS, moved into financial services, and incorporated services into major product areas.[20] For example, GE's engine contracts are not designed for selling engines as a product, but for selling a "guaranteed level of engine uptime for the contracted period, including parts, repairs, replacement engines, financing—whatever it takes to make the plane fly."[21]

Even Procter & Gamble is testing a move into services. In an Atlanta test market, a company named Juvian will collect and deliver laundry, allowing consumers to choose from a menu of unique spa treatments resulting in clothes feeling "indescribably luxurious." Juvian will also perform other services such as dry cleaning, upholstery cleaning, personal laundry consultation, or a comparison of the costs of doing laundry at home versus the cost of Juvian's services.[22]

"Organizations are starting to reorganize themselves around knowledge."

Dan Rasmus, Vice President, Giga Information Group, *Consumer Goods Technology,* Oct. 2000

Changing the direction of a company, incorporating new products, or developing a service mentality are all decisions that must be based upon trends in the marketplace, changing consumer needs, and available technology. Manufacturers need information from the marketplace **and** about end consumers, emerging technologies, and new product development activities to balance competing demands and forge the future direction of their companies.

With this information and continuous feedback from partners and intermediaries, companies can choose to introduce products and services that add value to consumers and create profit for the company. Continuous information gathering, focus on consumers, making decisions consistent with company goals, and vigilance over costs in a collaborative environment are the key ingredients for suppliers' success. Companies that fail to recognize the changing wants and needs of the consumer are doomed to failure!

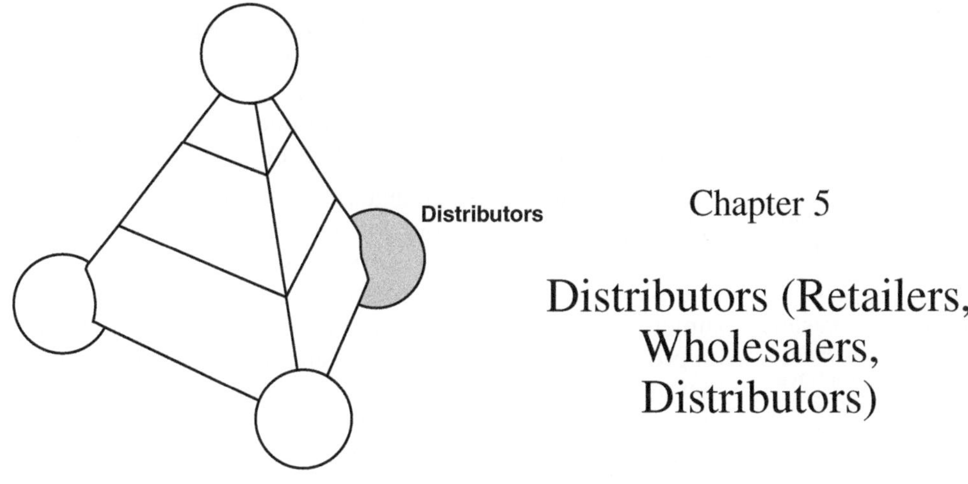

Chapter 5

Distributors (Retailers, Wholesalers, Distributors)

"In a strange sort of way, the final answer to all these questions—if indeed there is a final answer—will come from the consumer, who will decide where and when to shop and what to buy. Issues of independence and consolidation will matter not a whit, as long as the shopper is satisfied."

Kevin Coupe
IdeaBeat, January 2, 2001

Trying to classify types of retail formats today is very difficult. As grocery stores expand their pharmacy sections and free standing pharmacy stores expand their food sections, the lines of distinction blur. Kroger now operates department and jewelry stores as well as grocery and "marketplace" stores. Ahold now operates a food service organization in the United States as well as grocery stores. PETsMART sells may of the same products that are sold at Wal-Mart or Kmart. Convenience stores expanded and now offer an assortment of prod-

"[I]n today's markets, the retailer adds no value . . . by buying and reselling nationally branded products as they are."

Glen Terbeek,
Agentry Agenda,
1999

ucts similar to the corner grocery stores of years past. Specialty stores in the mall, such as Williams Sonoma or Nine West, compete with merchandise sold in department stores. Warehouse clubs, originally developed to serve small businesses, now sell full-line groceries to members. The limited assortment store has increased dramatically in popularity over the past few years (see Table 5.1).

"[C]onsumers today have to contend with a shopping experience shaped by a distribution infrastructure and marketing strategies that have developed since the 1960s, and that no longer meet the needs of shoppers who have too little time and too much data."

Bruce Westbrook, Deloitte & Touche, *MMR,* Feb. 19, 2001

In the midst of these changes, owners and managers of retail outlets have been under considerable pressure to increase revenues and reduce costs. Grocery stores found themselves in a particularly difficult position in the early 1990s. Consumers did not significantly increase the total amount spent on groceries (see Table 5.2). Consumers did, however, spend that money across a greater variety of retail outlets. The long-term viability of this industry depended upon finding ways to lower operating expenses and add **value** to the consumer.

Some of the alternative formats, such as the club stores and discount drugstores, had been successful in finding ways to operate with much lower operating expenses. In 1992 and 1993, retailers, manufacturers, distributors, brokers, and industry associations in the grocery and consumer packaged goods (CPG) industry in the United States came together to examine the state of their industry. In January 1993, the results of the Kurt Salmon Associates study, *ECR—Efficient Consumer Response: Enhancing Consumer Value in the*

TABLE 5.1. Consumers Who Shop Pretty Much Every Time or Fairly Often at Various Alternative Formats

Type of Store	1999 (%)	2000 (%)	2001 (%)	2002 (%)
Discount Stores	22	26	28	28
Warehouse Club Stores	10	14	14	16
Low-Price, No-Frills	X	11	13	10

Source: FMI reported in Ghitelman, David (2001), "Rush to Retail," *Supermarket News* (September 17), pp. 9, 12-13; *Trends in the United States: Consumer Attitudes and the Supermarket,* Washington, DC: Food Marketing Institute, 2002.

TABLE 5.2. Weekly Family Grocery Expenses (in 2001 dollars)

1996	1997	1998	1999	2000	2001	2002
$95	$93	$95	$94	$90	$94	$87

Source: FMI reported in Ghitelman, David (2001), "Rush to Retail," *Supermarket News* (September 17), pp. 9, 12-13; *Trends in the United States: Consumer Attitudes and the Supermarket, 2002.* Washington, DC: Food Marketing Institute, 2002.

Grocery Industry, were published, indicating that $30 billion could be saved and 41 percent less inventory would be required if inefficiencies in the system were eliminated.[1] The study identified four major areas for cost savings: $4.2 billion in Efficient Assortment, $11.4 billion in Efficient Promotion, $2.5 billion in Efficient Product Development, $11.9 billion in Efficient Replenishment. This new business paradigm was called Efficient Consumer Response (ECR) and defined as a responsive, consumer-driven system in which distributors and suppliers work together to maximize customer satisfaction and minimize cost.

"There is an awful lot of waste both in cost and responsiveness in today's supply chain. The only way to really tackle that is to begin operating the supply chain as one."

Ralph Drayer,
Retired Vice President
of Procter & Gamble,
IdeaBeat
June 8, 2001

By examining the whole supply chain as one integrated process, by having all supply chain partners communicate with one another, and by keeping the ability to better meet the needs of the end consumer as the goal, the system could operate more efficiently and everyone would win: manufacturers, retailers, consumers, and shareholders (Win-Win-Win-Win). However, this new paradigm required a change in business practices and is predicated on the assumption that a sale occurs when a consumer purchases the product off of a retail shelf. Instead of focusing on how to buy products with a good margin and store them until needed, the new approach is to offer the appropriate assortment of products and order replenishment for what consumers actually purchase!

This new paradigm resulted in a flurry of work: pilot studies, assessments of new business practices, and the publication of more than forty Best Practices books. These books examine specific areas, such as Activity Based Costing, Efficient Assortment, Category Management, etc., describing

"The philosophies of ECR have become ingrained in the industry. That is perhaps the best legacy of the initiative."

Michael Sansolo
Senior Vice President, FMI,
Supermarket News,
March 6, 2002

the current best practices based upon an evaluation of new ways of sharing information, measuring activities, and evaluating performance. The books also describe the amount of time required to get started and proficient in a particular task, the investment required, and the length of time needed for recouping the investment. Many of the specific practices and processes will be discussed in the third section of this book.

A NEW BUSINESS PARADIGM

This new business paradigm spawned new software, hardware, business processes, accounting processes, human resource policies, marketing activities, and management processes. How does the owner or manager of a retail outlet evaluate and choose among all these tools, techniques, and practices? Retailers need to focus on four areas:

1. Develop a clearly articulated mission and strategy.
2. Adopt collaborative business processes.
3. Obtain knowledge about consumers and the marketplace.
4. Decide which tools are needed to accomplish your mission.

MISSION AND STRATEGY

"94 of the top 100 department store chains of 1969 are gone now."

Peter Gertler
Deloitte Consulting
MMR, Feb. 21, 2001

Each retail organization needs to carve out its own position in the minds of consumers. Are you the retail outlet that comes to mind when consumers think of high fashion? sports equipment? health food? baby furniture? a "stock up" shopping trip? jewelry? quick trip for milk or bread? a gift item? children's clothes? Are you the retail outlet with everyday low prices or the one with the best sale this week?

Wal-Mart has the image of the everyday low price discount store. Prices are always kept low and consumers go there to buy everything from hardware items to paint to shoes to kitchen items to music to jewelry to groceries. By creating supply chain efficiencies and collaborative relationships with suppliers that include sharing information about consumers, Wal-Mart is able to offer products at low prices.

Target positions itself as the upscale discount store by offering a variety of products at relatively low prices but offering upscale or trendy designs, colors, and brand names. For instance, Target partnered with Eddie Bauer to create a line of modern, high quality camping gear and accessories to expand the outdoor sports department.[2] Kohl's also creates a unique middle approach with the cost structure of a discounter and the brands of a department store. Instead of an everyday low price strategy, Kohl's relies heavily on promotions while offering a convenient shopping experience with no surprises.[3]

These three successful retail organizations all position themselves differently in the marketplace, but each one has a clear mission and strategy. When confronted with new technologies, new business processes, and new techniques, the successful companies on the superhighway choose to adopt only those technologies, processes, and techniques that are consistent with and support their mission and strategy. Part of this new business paradigm is the collaborative approach to business.

COLLABORATION

Collaboration involves sharing information, developing joint strategies, or establishing electronic linkages. One of the major types of software used in these collaborations by retailers and manufacturers is Collaborative Planning, Forecasting, and Replenishment (CPFR). Versions of this software are being used by retailers and manufacturers in a variety of industries, such as Kmart, Ace Hardware, Best Buy, Canadian Tire, Hewlett-Packard, Kimberly-Clark, and Schering-Plough.

Several retail outlets created working relationships with Internet companies to address the issues of inventory, distribution, and technology. Ahold's online efforts have reached breakeven in the Netherlands and are close to breakeven in Argentina. Ahold acquired Peapod.com. Both partners had expertise that was valuable to the other side—Ahold has strong front-end knowledge and Peapod.com has expertise in interactive marketing. While Ahold predicted a profit from its online activity in the United States in 2001, that did not happen. Ahold lost $32.2 million on its online activity in 2001.[4] Amazon.com has partnerships with Toys "R" Us and Target. The partnerships enable Amazon.com to expand the product categories it offers. Toys "R" Us and Target are able to combine Amazon.com's technological expertise with their existing stores and distribution capabilities.

Forms of collaboration will be discussed in more detail in the third section of the book. Examples of collaborative activities are provided throughout the book to demonstrate the pervasiveness of this new business process.

CONSUMER AND MARKETPLACE KNOWLEDGE

Successful retailers need to know who their consumers are, what they want, how they want to purchase products or services, AND how they change. At the same time, retailers need to keep abreast of the changing technology and business processes that are being developed. Strategies can then be modified in ways that keep the retail outlet on track with its mission.

Consumer Knowledge

Technology is available to do anything you want in terms of data collection, sorting, analysis, or transmission. More than forty books describe best practices for implementing business processes. Incorporating the tools and practices that will have the most positive impact on your business involves choosing those tools and processes that enable your company to most effectively accomplish its mission.

For example, if you are trying to provide a particular group of consumers with the best prices then you might concentrate on those tools and processes that increase your efficiency. If you are trying to provide your consumers with the best selection you might concentrate on the tools and processes that help determine the best assortment of products.

If you know where you are going and what your company is trying to achieve with which group of consumers, then you can review the wealth of choices, information, suggestions, and recommendations available to determine which tools and processes will be most appropriate for your company. No two companies have precisely the same mission or objectives. No two companies will want to use the same tools or processes because they are not trying to achieve the same goals. Choosing the tools to best accomplish your mission is the key to success.

Chapter 2 described the demassification of the marketplace, changing consumer demographics and needs, and the need to understand the multidimensional nature of consumers. This section examines the changing nature of consumers with regard to purchasing products and services from retail outlets. In general, consumers are making fewer trips to the grocery store or mall and are spending less time shopping while there. So, how do you get them to come to your store and how do you get them to make purchases while there? The first step is understanding who your consumers are and what they want.

"If supermarkets don't begin to offer what the customer is asking for, which is prepared foods, they won't be around much longer."

Brian Sodus, *Marketing News,* May 20, 1996

Over the past five years, the amount of money spent weekly on groceries by families has remained essentially the same (see Table 5.2). However, the retail outlet varied. In addition, consumers shop at different retail formats for different reasons (see Table 5.3). While many consumers (66 percent) shop at grocery stores to stock up on groceries, almost half of the consumers (45 percent) go to discount stores for savings. While about a third of consumers (39 percent) shop at a grocery store for convenience items, about a third also shop at convenience stores (38 percent) and discount stores (34 percent) for those items. Depending upon your mission and strategy, you need to determine which consumers you want coming to your store for what kinds of products.

TABLE 5.3. Why Consumers Shop for Groceries at Various Formats*

Format	Convenience Items (%)	Stock Up on Groceries (%)	Stock Up on Nonfood Items (%)	Specialty Items (%)	Savings Discounts (%)	Never Shop at This Kind of Store (%)
Convenience Store	38	2	5	6	6	33
Discount Store	34	15	33	25	45	7
Drugstore	24	5	18	25	19	31
Supermarket	39	66	21	20	36	2
Warehouse Club	7	17	15	9	24	53

Source: FMI reported in Ghitelman, David (2001), "Rush to Retail," *Supermarket News* (September 17), pp. 9, 12-13; *Trends in the United States: Consumer Attitudes and the Supermarket, 2001.* Washington, DC: Food Marketing Institute, 2001.

*Numbers do not add up to 100 percent because multiple answers accepted.

"The consumer has spoken and two-thirds say they don't like going to the grocery store."

Robert Brindle, Nabisco, *Executive Technology,* April 2001

When consumers choose a particular grocery store, or convenience store, or discount store, what criteria are important to them? One study of grocery stores found that price was only one reason why consumers choose a particular store and not even the criterion chosen most often (see Table 5.4). Price is certainly part of the value equation but is only one of several variables in the equation. Each retail outlet needs to determine which variables are part of the value equation for its customers and how important each variable is.

Owners of small independent stores have generally known which consumers preferred which products and understood their purchasing habits. However, large retail outlets find it much more difficult to keep track of this information—managers don't know all of their consumers personally, don't

TABLE 5.4. Why Do Consumers Pick a Store?

Criterion	**Percentage**
Clean/neat	95
Quality produce	90
Quality meat	88
Courteous employees	82
Low price	78
Convenient location	77

Source: Food Marketing Institute (1996), *The Food Marketing Industry Speaks* (May 6), Chicago, IL: Food Marketing Institute.

know each consumer's preference, and don't always know the purchasing cycles of their consumers.

Since most retail outlets now use scanners, a wealth of information about what products are purchased when and in what quantity is available. If you have cards that identify consumers you can even determine which households buy what products in what quantity. Analyzing these data will provide valuable information about how often consumers shop, what day of the week they shop, when they come to stock up on items versus when they come to purchase specific items, what products are purchased frequently in small quantities, or what combinations of products are purchased during a single trip.

"At the end of the day, they (consumer) want more value, quality products, good service in a shopping environment that has more than low prices. Price competition is diminishing as motivation to shop a store."

Ed Comeau, Vice President, Donaldson, Lufkin and Jenrette, *Progressive Grocer,* March 1999

These data mining activities are even more valuable when trading partners share information. The Grocery Manufacturers Association and PriceWaterhouseCoopers found that an effective partnership between a manufacturer and retailer sharing and analyzing information could increase brand sales more than 10 percent and improve combined gross margin dollars on specific product categories.[5] Mining the data for relationships among consumers and their purchases provides deeper consumer insights that can lead to more precise marketing activities.

A number of retail outlets have developed their own Web sites for online shopping as another option for their consumers to use when purchasing goods and services. Some retailers created Web sites to develop a more cost-effective way to sell to consumers. Boston Consulting Group found that it costs $7 to market to existing consumers via the Web versus $34 to acquire a new Web consumer.[6] Consumers have a variety of reasons for shopping online (see Table 5.5). Again, price is an important criterion for some consumers, but not necessarily the reason given most often. One characteristic of consumers who shop online is that speed is important to them. BizRate found that 60 percent of the online shopping Web sites do not even use automatic acknowledgments of orders and that only 30 percent have customer support providing e-mail responses within twenty-four hours. One Harris survey found that customer satisfaction with online shopping drops dramatically if customers have not had a response within the first twenty-four hours.

Whether you capture data from an online Web site, from scanner data, from an independent marketing research firm, or from a manufacturer, you can use the information to better understand the needs of different consumers. For instance, you might find that some consumers replenish dog food monthly or that some consumers used to buy paper products at your store but have stopped or that those consumers who purchased beginning stages baby food this week will be pur-

TABLE 5.5. Top Reasons for Shopping Online

Reason	Percentage
I can shop during off hours.	74
It saves time.	68
It saves trips to the mall or the store.	67
I can shop at stores I cannot visit where I live.	66
I find better prices online.	57
I can shop without salesperson pressure.	54
I can compare products more easily	50

Source: "Convenience Simplified" (2000), *USA Today* (November).

chasing baby juice packets in another six weeks or that some consumers buy all their baby items at your store except diapers. Product assortment decisions, replenishment decisions, and marketing communication strategies can be based on this information.

"The typical American shopper now uses no fewer than three different frequent shopper cards."

David Pinto, Editor, *MMR,* March 20, 2000

Retailers want to build loyalty to their stores and one of the programs initiated by many retailers is the use of loyalty cards. According to Deloitte and Touche, 64 percent of retail leaders in the United States use loyalty cards. However, most consumers have a number of "loyalty cards" so they can take advantage of the savings offered by different retail outlets. Consumers may be frustrated having to carry so many cards and keep track of when they have purchased five items to get the sixth one free, or whether they have purchased the right number of items within the allotted time frame to get their special gift or savings. In many cases the loyalty cards are cumbersome for consumers to keep track of and use.

"Wal-Mart doesn't have a loyalty program because we don't believe in discriminating between customers. We wouldn't offer one customer a better value than we offer another customer."

Kevin Turner, Vice President, Wal-Mart, *Chain Store Age,* July 1999

Loyalty cards enable retailers to analyze purchase data by household. With this kind of data one independent retailer realized that providing a standardized discount for all consumers visiting the store did not tailor the plan to individual consumers. By not providing for their individual lifestyles, needs, and tastes, a generic loyalty card offering a discount on items selected by the retailer or manufacturer does not necessarily meet consumers' needs. So this retailer used S&H Greenpoints and provided consumers with a catalog from which gifts could be chosen.[7] Each receipt gave the current total of Greenpoints so consumers could easily keep track of how many points had been acquired. Looking in the catalog, consumers could see how close they were to getting an item they desired and would plan to return to the store to acquire the desired number of points. In addition, the retailer could identify how valuable individual consumers were. On Valentine's Day, the top 500 consumers received a dozen long-stemmed red roses.

Another independent retailer used software to collect and track consumers' specific purchases and designed a loyalty program. By tailoring marketing activities to appeal directly to the most profitable consumers or to encourage less profitable consumers to purchase more products or more often, the outlet generated a $630,000 improvement in profits.[8]

Some retail outlets are developing branded private labels as a way to create loyal customers. To make this strategy work you have to know your consumers, know what they want, and decide what role private label brands will play. If you have provided a product that satisfies the consumers and they want to purchase it again, they have to come back to your outlet. The only place to buy Arizona jeans is JCPenney; the only place to purchase Private Selection is a Kroger-owned store. If consumers become loyal to a private label, they also become loyal to a particular retailer.

Just as the local store owners knew their consumers, their tastes, and their purchasing habits, so too can today's retailers have that same knowledge. Size makes it impossible for any one store owner or manager to store all of the information in his or her head. Therefore, software that collects relevant information in a format that allows the retailer to develop that same level of understanding is critical. After all, your consumers are your most important assets.

Market Knowledge

According to the University of Michigan Business School's American Consumer Satisfaction Index, the overall rating of customer satisfaction with retail establishments—including department and discount stores, supermarkets, fast-food restaurants, and gas stations—dropped 0.5 percent in the fourth quarter of 2000. Satisfaction with supermarkets declined 1.4 percent.[9] In a longitudinal study, Andersen Consulting reported that 73 percent of shoppers ranked Internet shopping as the highest in terms of overall satisfaction compared to brick and mortar stores (60 percent) and catalogs (56 percent).[10] These findings, along with the statistics showing that consumers shop less often and spend less time in stores and that many consumers prefer shopping online, indicate that retailers need to think about why consumers do not find shopping in stores to be as satisfactory as in the past.

A number of retailers are rethinking the shopping experience and beginning to experiment with alternative formats and/or new features. One approach is to make retail outlets **"family friendly."** This approach ranges from providing special parking places for expectant mothers to providing extra seats that strap onto the back of carts to provide extra room to adding a location where children can color, draw, or play with toys. Some retailers provide electric powered carts for senior citizens or child-sized grocery carts or child seats that resemble racing cars. These features are all aimed at making it more convenient and more fun for all members of the family when at the store.

FMI indicates that 70 percent of purchase decisions are made in the store.[11] Given this assumption, experimenting with ways to interact with consumers while they are shopping has significant implications for personalizing the shopping experience.

Some retailers are experimenting with the **use of technology** to provide consumer information and promotions. For example, Hy-Vee installed a wireless in-store network that was connected to a number of specially equipped carts. By using the monitors on the cart, consumers could find the location of specific items within the store, get news or weather, access special promotions, or make comparisons between private label and manufacturer brands. A plan for the future is that consumers would receive notices about specials that have been personalized for them based upon their history of purchases when their personal code has been entered into the retailer's system.

3Com, Apple, Compaq, Intel, Lucent Technologies, NEC, and Philips are among the vendors working on home networking products. Some combination of PCs, TVs, digital cameras, printers, and appliances will be networked and connected with the Internet. Consumers can order or have products replenished by either placing an order with a specific retail outlet or by having their networked device automatically contact a specified retailer to replenish a product. Consumers can organize recipes on their PCs, use a specific recipe organizer device, or can go to a retailer's Web page (such as Kroger's) to search for a recipe. Kitchen appliances are being modified to include scanning devices so that items being added to the shelves are recorded, empty containers can be scanned, and requests for replenishments are sent to a specific retail outlet.[12]

Personal digital assistants and the potential of wireless broadband technology provide the possibility for consumers to place orders for clothes, toys, groceries, or packaged goods or make appointments for hair cuts, oil changes, or delivery times from any location. Retailers would also have the possibility to communicate directly with individual consumers when a shipment of a favorite item arrives or when a special offer is available.

"Innovative shopping experiences and products will win the loyalty (and increased business) of individual shoppers."

Glen Terbeek, *Agentry Agenda*, 1999

Since the experience of shopping is an important part of the value equation and since consumers are not entirely satisfied with their shopping experience, a number of retailers are experimenting with major **changes in format.** Albertson's, for example, compares the shopping experience to theater and works from the assumption that the ambiance of the store has a dramatic impact on consumers' evaluation of the entire store. One of Albertson's new stores has departments, such as "Beverage Boulevard" or "Snack Central," with accompanying lights and graphics to create a small town streetscape. Appealing to a more complete sensory experience, some of the Albertson's stores have "scratch bakeries" with the aroma of fresh bread, cookies, or cakes floating throughout the store.[13]

"Consumers want fresh products. . . . They want fresh tortillas and salsa. They want wasabi. They want sushi. They want the kinds of things they've had in restaurants."

David Bennett, Co-owner of Mill Valley, *Supermarket News*, March 26, 2001

A variety of attempts have been made to make the shopping experience more fun, to appeal to all the senses, and to generate excitement. Wegman's has added an extrawide fresh food aisle that comprises nearly one-third of the total selling floor space. The patisserie, boulangerie (fresh Artisan breads), and gourmet cheese sections include demonstrations by chefs, sampling of new items and freshly made products. Dorothy Lane in Dayton is famous for its "killer" brownies. They sell for $1.99 each. Dorothy Lane sells 4,000 to 5,000 every week. V. Richards opened a "fresh meals store" with packaged single-serving entrées, side dishes, and desserts. In each case, the retailer is creating excitement, creating a particular image for its store, and establishing itself as a destination for consumers.

Grocery stores are not the only retail outlets moving in this direction. In January 2001, Steve Jobs remarked, "Buying a car is no longer the worst purchasing experience; buying a computer is now number one." By the following summer the first Apple retail stores opened their doors with a specific goal in mind: "Visit the Apple store to learn something new, test drive a Mac or spark your creativity. It'll be a shopping experience that's every bit as rewarding as using a Mac itself." Inside these stores, everything from digital cameras to MP3 players to PDAs to computers (iMacs, G4 Towers, Powerbooks, and iBooks) are on display, are hooked up, and work. Consumers are encouraged to try the equipment: they can listen to music, experiment with iMovie, burn CDs, watch demonstrations in the movie theater, or even have questions answered by an expert at the "Genius Bar."[14] Like the new grocery store concepts, the retail store is being designed as a destination for consumers where they can engage in activity and experience the products. Consumers need a good reason to visit the store.

When expanding the concept to other countries, retailers need to realize that it will not happen quickly and that not all concepts translate equally well to other cultures. When Wilson's set out to open a branch of The Leather Experts in a London airport, they anticipated that it would take two months. The actual time to opening was six months.[15] Adaptation of products, space, and business issues such as taxes all take time to understand, find the most effective form, and implement.

Wal-Mart had some difficulty in Germany when announcing price cuts on 1,000 items in an attempt to win sales and market share as well as establish its position as the retailer with everyday low prices. The German Cartel Office, however, ordered Wal-Mart, Aldi, and Lidi to stop selling basic food items below cost. The German government views its relationship with business differently than the U.S. government. The intention of the U.S. government is to ensure a level playing field for conducting business and ensuring that companies do not collaborate or operate as monopolies in ways that would be harmful to consumers. The German government, on the other hand, believes that a short-term benefit to the consumer (such as lower prices) does not make up for the long-term harm done to the competitive retail climate within the country.[16]

Measurement and Performance

"We're moving information today; we're not moving cases anymore."

Mike Bergmann, Director, Warehousing and Distribution, Wegman's, *Supermarket News,* Oct. 15, 2001

This new collaborative, consumer-centric business paradigm involves major changes in business processes, practices, and policies. Companies need flexibility to adapt to changing consumer needs, emerging technologies, and collaborative activities. Employees need to change their day-to-day work behavior to accommodate changing business processes. Current metrics for company and/or employee performance do **not** result in flexible or changed behaviors.

If desired business processes and performance under this new paradigm are different from the past, new metrics for measuring performance are required. Companies respond to requests for information, complaints, or orders, or to determine customer satisfaction, loyalty, and profitability. In addition to measuring their own individual performances, companies also need to measure how they accomplish these goals when working collaboratively with other companies. Those issues and concerns are relevant for all organizations, are major issues, and require a great deal of focus and attention. In Section III, Chapter 8 examines the internal processes in more depth and Chapter 9 examines the collaborative processes in more depth.

"Yesterday's conventional wisdom and rational answers no longer work for today's besieged food industry—and tomorrow is even less predictable."

Ryan Matthews, *Progressive Grocer*

Many opportunities for change are available to retailers: expansion in other countries, new technology, new product or service offerings, alternative store formats, or potential partnerships. Deciding that not all of these choices are right for your outlet is easy. Deciding which choices will work for your outlet is not so easy. You need to answer the following questions first:

- What do you want your retail outlet to stand for? What image do you want it to project? How should it function in consumers' lives?
- Who are your consumers? What do they expect from a visit to your store?
- Which consumers are most profitable or valuable to you? What are their characteristics?
- What makes consumers different? Can you personalize products, services, or communication with your consumers?
- Where and how do you add **VALUE** to the consumer?

Staying abreast of new developments is important. However, you don't need to try them all. Once you have identified your mission and goal, when you have analyzed all the consumer data available to you, when you understand consumer similarities and differences, and after you understand the needs of your most valuable or profitable consumers, then you can choose the technology and formats that will work best for your outlet. Technologies become "tools" or "enablers" that help assist in accomplishing your mission.

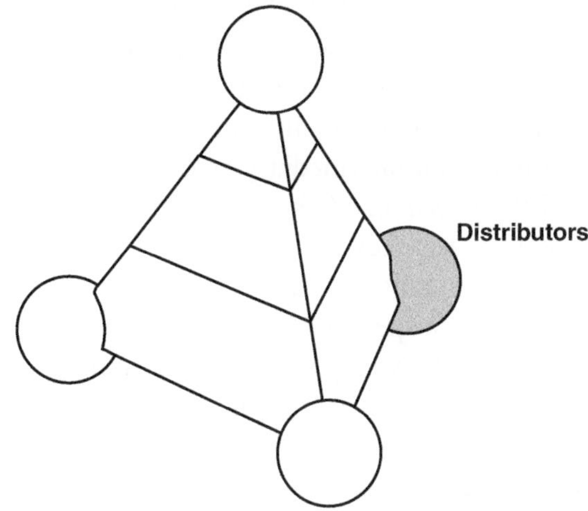

Chapter 6

Intermediaries (Brokers, Agents)

"For AGENTS . . . it means providing the best shopping experience, whether through new formats, solution selling, private label, more value-added services, 'consumer direct' market channels, and many other innovations."

Glen Terbeek
Agentry Agenda

"Like fashion retailers who use 'personal shoppers' for their best customers, an **AGENT** knows all about a customer's preferences; the **AGENT** could suggest complementary merchandise, and the shopper would trust the **AGENT'S** recommendations."

Glen Terbeek,
Agentry Agenda

Businesses and consumers can purchase products and services from any company in their immediate geographic area or from any company that has a Web site on the Internet. The array of choices is mind-boggling. Trying to evaluate the reliability of each company, product, or service is an overwhelming task. One response in the face of this daunting task is to simply order nothing. Another response is to rely on name-brand products, services, and outlets. Another response is to take the time to research every product, service, or outlet before placing an order. Another response is to purchase from whatever outlet has the lowest price. Another response is to put your faith in a third-party source who will take the time to sort through the offerings available and make recommendations or provide evaluations of alternatives.

"[N]ew exchanges such as yet2.com and the Patent and License Exchange (plx.com) . . . seek to create whole new venues to buy, sell, and license ideas and intellectual property."

Amy Cortese, "Masters of Innovation," *Business Week,* March 23, 2001

The last choice represents the use of an intermediary. An intermediary helps consumers or organizations by providing convenient, easy access to products, information, and solutions. You might think of an intermediary as *Consumer Reports* on steroids. Like *Consumer Reports,* the intermediary may evaluate products, services, or retail outlets. Unlike *Consumer Reports,* intermediaries can be proactive—they can direct the consumer to a specific store or Web site where a purchase can be made or they may even offer the ability for the consumer to purchase directly from the intermediary's site. In addition, some of the intermediaries just help consumers or businesses interact when their partners use different forms of technology. This is a new interactive business form and, as such, there are many variations—from a "Personal Shopper" hired to shop for you, to an electronic exchange on the Internet evaluating opportunities for you, to an Internet site that facilitates shopping by offering you limited choices. Intermediaries are equally important in business in business-to-business (B2B) or business-to-consumer (B2C) situations. In both cases, the intermediaries **provide value** by facilitating transactions.

The purpose of an intermediary may be to do one or several of the following activities:

1. anticipate and deliver value to the consumer,
2. capture a consumer's "moment of desire" to benefit both the consumer and manufacturer,
3. resolve uncertainty by providing ready access to information and solutions, or
4. make it easy to restock shelves with staples.[1]

A particular intermediary may perform one, several, or all four functions.

EVALUATION

Some Web sites will now identify outlets where the product is available or the price charged at specific outlets; some Web sites also evaluate products or retail outlets. For example, Cnet.com provides product reviews for computer hardware, electronics, and software. Each of the products receives a score from one to ten along with a description of features and an evaluation of good and bad points. Visitors to the Web site can request comparisons of specific products and can also find the price of the products. For those consumers with limited knowledge of manufacturers, products, or criteria for evaluation, cnet.com offers a valuable service. The task of having to track down the the Web site of every manufacturer, read the description of each product, develop the criteria for evaluating choices, examine each product, and find reviews of each product has already been accomplished. After reviewing products at this site, consumers can make more educated decisions about which products best suit their needs.

"The new networked competitors will have started with the Internet as a tool for integrating the operations of a network of companies."

Patrick L. Kiernan, President, Day/Kiernan & Associates, *Food Logistics*

Cdnet.com and zdnet.com offer a slightly different service. When consumers already know what product they wish to purchase, cdnet.com and zdnet.com offer a valuable service for hardware, software, or electronics. Once a consumer identifies a specific product, cdnet.com will list stores (retail or Web site) from which the product can be purchased along with the price being charged for the product at each location. Consumers can then find the least expensive retail outlet or the retail outlet with which they have done business in the past and had a satisfactory experience. If the consumer happens to be unfamiliar with the retail outlets listed, cdnet.com offers one more service: each of the retail outlets is given a rating. Using this Web site, consumers can balance the purchase price against the reliability of the retail outlet and make a choice about which outlet to use . . . **the consumer's choice is not always just about price!**

"Sam Walton raised us to understand that the customer is the boss, and Wal-Mart buyers are agents for the customer."

Wal-Mart, *Supermarket News*, Nov. 5, 2001

Some of the B2B exchanges are acting as a portal, offering a variety of services for companies. For instance, some exchanges are a portal providing services that convenience stores need, such as back office systems, the purchase order processes, the ability to participate in auctions, or providing information.[2] Another type of intermediary is WebMD, whose goal is to create a seamless connection between doctors, patients, hospitals, and insurers as a way to streamline health care.[3] Regardless of the industry, intermediaries can play a vital role in delivering information, evaluating choices, and facilitating contacts.

SHOPPING EXPERIENCE

Manufacturers and retailers alike have introduced Web sites that allow consumers to purchase products directly. These sites are involved in both demand creation and demand fulfillment. In both cases, collaboration has been necessary.

Several manufacturers, such as Kraft, Nabisco, Quaker Oats, or Procter & Gamble, have individual pages on their Web sites devoted to specific products. While manufacturers may use these pages to offer consumer advice, such as what to do when your baby has diaper rash or nutritional information partnered with recipes, selling products directly to consumers may jeopardize current relationships with distributors and/or retailers. As a result, none of these manufacturers sells from a Web site products that are available in retail outlets.

However, if the Web sites work well, they create excitement for and interest in the products as well as the convenience of making a purchase. If consumers are ready to purchase, the manufacturers need to be able to capitalize on that desire to purchase. These manufacturers direct consumers interested in purchasing their products to NetGrocer.com.[4] In some cases, loyal consumers can purchase items no longer carried in retail outlets because of low sales. For example, it is still possible to purchase Sugar-Free Tang through the NetGrocer link on Kraft's Web site.

Some manufacturers offer products for sale only over the Internet. For example, Reflect.com is a Procter & Gamble

Web site that sells customized cosmetics to consumers only through its Web site. Once a consumer has registered, which includes completing a questionnaire that creates an individualized profile, the database keeps track of what that person orders. Periodically, each consumer receives notices about products that are either being offered at a special price, new products that are being introduced, or special promotions on products that the consumer has ordered previously. These types of Web sites assume the intermediary activities of creating and capturing the consumer's "moments of desire" as well as making it easy to keep staple items on hand.

Other Web sites work proactively as an intermediary to inform consumers of new products that might be of interest to them or to offer special promotions. Amazon.com or Barnes&Noble.com, for example, both use software that keeps track of consumer purchases and proactively sends e-mail messages to consumers letting them know of new titles that are available in their areas of interest or providing them with special offers.

Other retailers have joined forces with existing Internet companies to offer better value to consumers by creating better control over the demand creation and demand fulfillment processes. For instance, Amazon.com has a partnership with Toys "R" Us and Target. Both Toys "R" Us and Target can offer a broader array of products than is available at the Amazon.com Web site. Both Toys "R" Us and Target can offer better control over the Internet ordering and shipping process by employing the expertise of Amazon.com. All of the organizations benefit from the partnership and consumers have an easier time finding products of interest at either of the retailers' Web sites and ordering through the Web site and technology of Amazon.com.

"[I]n the 'Frictionless Marketplace' the 'value chain' is much more important than the supply chain."

Glen Terbeek, *Agentry Agenda*

INDUSTRY EXCHANGES

Some exchanges focus on providing value by offering greater control over the physical shipping of goods for both B2B and B2C conditions. For instance, Americold Logistics,

United States Cold Storage (USCS), Service Craft, and Total Logistic Control (TLC) track orders from the placement of an order, the facility from which the item is sourced, through the delivery process until the product reaches the consumer, and will even provide replenishment information to the companies involved.[5] Consumers and manufacturers have access to this information so they both know where the product is at all times, thereby allowing for maximum transparency and control.

"[B]ackhauling will continue to challenge the transportation industry, but admits that exchanges may play a role in making a complicated situation a bit simpler."

Dan Raftery, President, Prime Consulting Group, *Food Logistics,* April 15, 2001

Nistevo is an Internet-based forum for shippers and carriers to exchange information aimed at maximizing the number of trucks moving full loads of goods. Logistics.com is an Internet-based site that provides analysis and works as a liaison between shippers and carriers.[6] Both of these ventures are aimed at bringing organizations together for the purpose of exchanging information, developing better control over fulfillment processes, and creating additional efficiency.

For example, a typical manufacturer might work with only ten to 100 shippers. By having access to all 450,000 carriers, manufacturers would have more information and may be able to bring costs down dramatically.[7] In addition, an intermediary that tracks, schedules, and plans shipments online may also be able to provide backhauling opportunities, thereby eliminating the number of trucks that are empty on the return trip. The intermediary activities provided by these exchanges provide information, evaluate possible scheduling opportunities, and increase efficiency.

GlobalNetExchange is an online exchange for retailers and suppliers with backers such as Kroger, Carrefour, SA, MetroAG, J. Sainsbury, ColesMyer, Pinault-Printemps, Redoute, and Sears, Roebuck and Co.[8] In a partnership with TradingProduce.com, GlobalNetExchange provides access for its members to 270 suppliers of perishable products. This service fulfills the intermediary function of making all products available to the consumer.

GlobalNetExchange and Transora, online exchanges for about fifty manufacturing companies, are creating a megahub allowing interoperability among exchanges.[9] The megahub would facilitate cross-value chain applications such as Collaborative Planning, Forecasting, and Replenishment (CPFR), and joint promotions management. Transora, for example, purchased the online promotions company planet U to deliver promotions to targeted households over the Internet. These exchanges not only would make it easier to control purchases by retailers from manufacturers but would provide communication capabilities with end consumers. These exchanges continue to expand their role as intermediaries.

NEW FORMS

Intermediaries as proactive, interactive links among consumers, retailers, and manufacturers is a developing area. Services offered not only will reflect activities that have been done before, such as evaluation of products by *Consumer Reports,* but also will extend the intermediaries' reach into new forms of business. Napster is certainly one example. It originally provided a unique format for consumers to customize their choice of music. By challenging conventional wisdom, Napster has undergone criticism and legal challenges. In spite of these growing pains, Napster continued to pursue its goal and finally reached an agreement with the music industry. The form of Napster continues to change but it retains its intermediary function in a modified format.

Another type of intermediary exchange is one in which a pharmaceutical company and doctor can confer with a patient over a network to come up with a custom prescription plan. Working within this network, all parties are able to be part of the conversation and decision-making process. In this case, the pharmaceutical company is no longer selling drugs but is now selling a service, much like GE sells a service that includes providing an airplane engine. The pharmaceutical companies may sell the service of creating personalized choices of treatment and dosage.

Consumers today have an almost infinite number of choices available. Businesses have an almost infinite number of suppliers and/or buyers. As a result, information overload is real.

Trying to evaluate the quality of products is a real challenge with so many choices. Assessing the reputation of each outlet is also a challenge with so many choices. If there is an intermediary you trust, it will perform the evaluation for you, saving a tremendous amount of time and effort. For the intermediaries to be successful, they must establish and keep the trust of their consumers. When trust is established, intermediaries can expand into proactive activities, such as notifying consumers or companies of new product or service options. With an established relationship, intermediaries can offer more services **as long as they provide value for their consumers.**

Section III: Collaborative Business Processes

> "Significant shifts in the tools or methods that organizations deploy require four components before becoming the fabric of a new model. These components, technology, applications, standards, and culture must all migrate simultaneously, with a 'Darwin-like' selection process, toward a new way to conduct business."
>
> Richard A. Carman
> IdeaBeat.com, August 8, 2001

Previous chapters talked about the components of the business process: consumers, suppliers, distributors, and intermediaries. Suppliers, distributors, and intermediaries must all be involved in creating a seamless supply chain so consumers' changing needs can be met. To implement this business paradigm, companies must adopt new processes. This section will focus on the process: technology (what tools are necessary for implementing this process orientation), enablers (what processes are necessary to make the new paradigm work), and integrators (what processes are necessary for collaboration).

Remember, however, that this is **NOT** a program, **NOT** a project, **NOT** a system, and **NOT** just technology and **NOT** just another expense reduction. It **IS** a business process change—changing the way product flows, the way information flows, and the way cash flows. Literally, this new paradigm is about changing the way product is sourced, the way product is manufactured, the way it is transported, the processes of buying and selling, and the way product ultimately gets merchandised to the consumer.

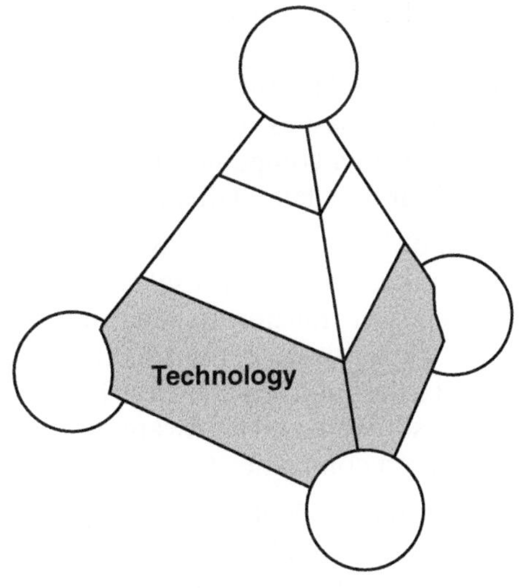

Chapter 7

Technology

"Companies have been led to believe that they could install vanilla-type software into an enterprise-wide environment and get customized results. The marketing has been that these systems are plug-and-play, basically. But that is just not so."

Steve Pratt
Global Leader for CRM Practice
Deloitte Consulting

The explosion of technology has been overwhelming—from space shuttles to laser instruments for surgery to cell phones that connect to the Internet to laptop computers under five pounds with more processing power than room-size computers had in the 1960s. Companies can find hardware and software to categorize, integrate, and analyze any data they choose to collect.

"I think there is a world market for maybe five computers."

Thomas Watson,
IBM, 1945

The new collaborative business paradigm companies need to exchange information with other companies to create an integrated, seamless supply chain. Each piece of hardware or software stores data in a different format, so exchanging data can be a nightmare. In addition, the output or reports may not be in a format that managers find useful for decision making. Complicating these technical issues are security concerns when exchanging data with other companies. Efficiencies are definitely possible and desirable, but challenges abound!

"Computing is not about computers any more. It is about living."

Nicholas Negroponte, *Being Digital,* 1995

A sophisticated piece of hardware, such as a lightweight handheld device for counting inventory, is useless if it cannot read the current UPC codes or transfer the data in a format that can be accepted by the software being used to compile information from several stores and warehouses. To be effective, companies must use software and hardware that is compatible within **AND** between companies (see Figure 7.1).

Before you even think about adopting this new business process, you must have a solid foundation of the right **hardware.** This could include scanning devices, computer systems, or radio frequency handhelds, among others. The middle illustration of the pyramid (Figure 7.1) addresses the need for the correct **infrastructure.** Included within the infrastructure concept is the need for standardization within industries and across countries. Examples would be UPCs (Universal Product Codes)/EANs (European Article Numbers) article numbers, common transaction codes for elec-

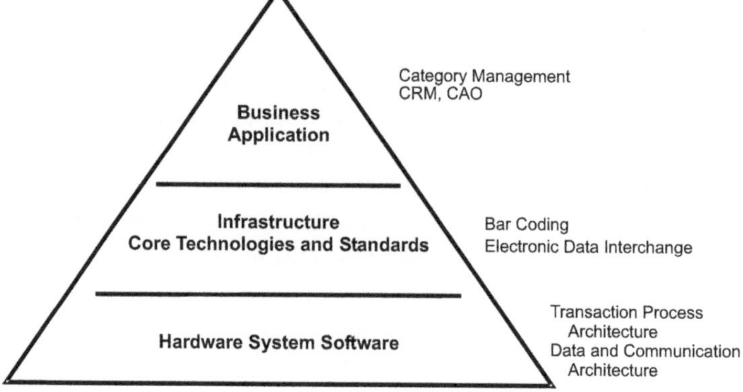

FIGURE 7.1. Layers of Technology

tronic data interchange (EDI), or pallet sizes. Once the first two levels are satisfied, then, and only then, can you begin to develop the **applications** that will support your business plan of implementing computer-assisted ordering, developing a warehouse management system, or using category management.

Choosing the best hardware and software that is compatible with your company's strategy is only part of the solution. Successful deployment is about 20 percent technology and 80 percent people. The culture of the organization—how people work, how they make decisions, how they treat consumers, how mission-driven the company is, how it integrates information, how it works with other organizations—determines how successful the use of hardware and software will be. This chapter addresses these three topics: hardware, standards, and business application.

HARDWARE

To be successful in an integrated and collaborative electronic environment, companies need to invest in hardware. Choosing when to purchase a particular type of hardware is not easy. According to Moore's Law, the numbers of transistors per integrated circuit would double every eighteen months.[1] Not only does the computing power increase, but also the price of hardware continues to fall. Deciding when to invest in a particular type of hardware is a difficult decision. Since personal computers often are outdated within two to three years, since the investment in hardware is significant, and since companies cannot afford to replace hardware often, making good choices is critical.

"Investments in technology can be significant and if not properly planned can be a barrier to achieving the optimal technology benefits."

ECR Technology Guide

The first requirement is to **acquire the hardware necessary** for collecting the transaction and consumer data and transmitting the required information to anyone in the organization when and where the data are needed. The second requirement is to acquire hardware that is capable of transmitting information among users. In a collaborative environment, you will be integrating your data into supplier, distributor, and intermediary systems, so choices must be made regarding the type of computers, networks, and form of data transmission.

- Should an investment be made in minicomputers or PCs?
- What type of network should be employed?
- Do all computers need to have access to all parts of the network?
- Should the network be dedicated or created on the Internet?
- Which hardware gives the appropriate level of privacy protection?
- Should connections be made over phone lines, a cable system, or satellite system?
- Should a wireless system be used?

This is an extremely expensive proposition! In some cases, the payback can create an excellent return on investment (ROI). In some cases, the payback does not materialize. For example, Nygard, a textile company, collected information from 300,000 consumers in 200 retail outlets. One of the problems Nygard has is that different retailers want to see the information laid out differently.[2] In the 1980s the automobile manufacturers each adopted their own computer-assisted design (CAD) systems. Suppliers were forced to have multiple systems in order to work with all the manufacturers. Investing in different systems certainly reduced the cost-effectiveness of the hardware investment.

Finding hardware or software that can adapt to many different system requirements is time-consuming and expensive and may not even be possible. Purchasing several forms of hardware or software is inefficient, can be cost prohibitive, and certainly reduces ROI.

Many companies are reluctant to invest in new hardware systems because there is always another new system that will do more for less. Instead, they invest in hardware and software that will try to integrate current hardware systems to perform the same functions advertised by the newer hardware systems or to connect with a new hardware system. Eventually, these companies find themselves spending so much time and money keeping the patchwork system working that they could have purchased a completely new system.

"You'll never make dramatic progress unless you engineer around legacy systems and legacy people."

Robert J. Herbold, Executive Vice President, Microsoft, *Supermarket News,* April 2, 2001

Development of the Internet facilitated the use of technology, especially when searching for or sharing information. The use of Internet technology in business situations not only involves other companies, but consumers as well. By the year 2000, 51 percent of U.S. households had a computer and 41.5 percent of U.S. households were connected to the Internet.[3] By the year 2000, there were about 315 million Internet users—about 5 percent of the world population.[4] Access to information, resources, and companies gives consumers newfound power. They can switch from one product manufacturer to another or from one retailer to another with the click of a mouse.

"Our estimate is that by the year 2010, we're going to see a one millionfold increase in the amount of information on the Internet."

Mike Nelson, Director of Internet Technology & Strategy, IBM, May 31, 2001

Many companies have created or are creating Web sites. In the consumer packaged goods (CPG) industry, 80 percent of the manufacturers have Web sites; however, not all Web sites perform similar functions.[5] Stage 1 of Web site development involves presenting information about the company, its products and services. Stage 2 Web sites allow consumers to make purchases online. Stage 3 Web sites are interactive, enabling consumers and business partners to ask questions or share information. All of the CPG Web sites surveyed presented information about the company and its products or services (Stage 1). However, only 49 percent use the Web sites to collect consumer feedback and only 30 percent use it to recruit employees. Only 30 percent conduct transactions with retail consumers and suppliers and only 22 percent sell directly to consumers (Stage 2). Only a few collaborate interactively with suppliers (12 percent) and retail consumers (13 percent) (Stage 3). Only 8 percent synchronize data with their trading partners.

The step from using the Internet to display information to developing any type of interactivity is a major barrier. The hardware system requires a move from displaying information to creating an interactive system. This requires not only

"In other words, first change your business approach, then re-engineer the roles of the people in your company to support the new approach, then—and only then—implement CRM technology solutions."

"What Is Customer Relationship Management," Special Advertising Section, *Business Week,* July 3, 2000

an investment in equipment but also a reengineering of the organization. The Webmaster does not normally have the capability to answer substantive questions about products, departments, consumer accounts, and technical issues. How does Human Resources get requests for employment from the Web site? How do Customer Service Representatives get requests for updated product information? How does the Accounts Receivable department get inquiries from the Web site? Once the right person receives the request, does that person have access to the right consumer files and company files so answers can be provided in a timely manner? Which individuals in which partner companies have access to what data from your company files?

Choosing the appropriate hardware and software is always a challenge. Making this decision when the technology changes at a rapid-fire pace is even more challenging. The best approach is to choose the technology that enables your company to implement its mission in a way that provides value to your consumers.

"Customer satisfaction doesn't necessarily drop when a machine answers the phone. It drops when the customer can't shake the machine and get to the representative. If a call is picked up within six rings and a rep is fully handling the customer's call within a minute, automated call routing has no negative impact on customer satisfaction."

John Goodman, President, TARP, *Marketing Tools,* Jan./Feb. 1998

When consumers contact a company, they want to have their question, concern, or request answered as quickly as possible. What hardware and/or software system do you need to facilitate this process? Many choices are available. How do you choose? Interactive Voice Response (IVR) systems screen consumers and provide access to automated information. By using prerecorded messages that allow consumers to choose the department or service with which to be connected, JC-Penney was able to trim about twelve to fifteen seconds off the time required for each call and boosted employee productivity by almost 4 percent.[6] Computer Telephone Integration (CTI) systems integrate the phone and computer systems so that the customer representative sees a consumer's record about a half a second before there is voice connection. In this case, the consumer's file contains information about ordering, shipping, payment, and product specification information from several functional areas within the company. According to a survey of ninety-two companies with average monthly call volumes of one million, the companies reduced the overall cost of calls by 1 to 10 percent.[7] Today, consumers expect that the products and services received in the store, over the phone, or over the Internet will be the same.[8] After all, you are the same company in all three places, right? Some consumers expect that questions about a product, a service, a bill, or delivery can be answered equally well in person, over the phone, or on the Internet.

"If they shop with you offline, they expect to be able to take advantage of the same products and services online."

Gomez Associations Study, *Supermarket News,* April 2, 2001

Who are your consumers? Who do they want to talk to when they call the company? About what? How do they contact the company? Do you need a phone system or Web site that can direct the consumer to the person who has the right information? Can you integrate your company data so consumers' questions are answered in a timely manner? Do you need an integrated phone and computer system that allows any employee who needs consumer information to have access to it from any department within the company? Depending upon your consumers, your company's mission, your current resources, and your goals, you can choose the type of hardware/software combination that works for the system you are designing to interact with consumers.

For example, the CEO of Close Call Corp. realized that technology changes were necessary in 1995. In 1996 the company was planning to expand from six call centers to 116, implementing new, open switching systems in the new centers to enable automatic dialing and call routing. In addition, information systems was updating all of Close Call's internal management systems by deploying new human resources and general ledger software. The CEO expected the "can-do" culture that he had nurtured from the early days of the company to carry it though this period of exponential growth and technological changes. He believed that making all the systems changes—including building the data warehouse—in a very short time frame was just a matter of getting the right people for the job, according to a consultant. From the start, the data warehouse lacked a clearly defined business objective, mostly because the users had never asked for greater analytical abilities. From the CEO's point of view, the entire project was a fiasco. The anemic pilot was delivered four months later than the initial (highly unrealistic) deadline for the fully functional warehouse. Besides wasting money and time, the project cost Close Call 50 percent of its IS staff, about half of whom quit.

The collaborative business process requires data exchange among all the companies involved in a supply chain. When using Scan Based Trading (SBT), for instance, retailers only take ownership of an item and pay suppliers when it is scanned at the point of sale. Retailers pay suppliers based on daily point-of-sale (POS) scan data. Retailers and consumer goods companies (CGCs) both depend upon consumer sales to get paid. This system is expensive and time-consuming, but results have been positive. A GMA pilot study documented sales growth increases of 4 percent over control stores, with shrink remaining at acceptable levels.[9] In this type of situation consumers win because the in-stock levels of product are increased. Suppliers win because of reduced operating costs and improved sales. Retailers win because of reduced operating costs, reduced investment, and improved sales.

With the introduction of wireless technology, Internet access will be ubiquitous (see Figure 7.2). All members of the supply chain can access data from any location. When broadband technology is readily available, consumers and businesspeople will be able to transmit large files, video, and sophisticated graphics from anywhere to anywhere. Which hardware and software will allow for data exchange among supply chain members? How can incompatible systems be made compatible? What security measures are available? Who will have access to which data? The best approach is to identify the business processes that will be involved, the data requirements for those processes, the people and functions involved in the process, and the objectives to be met. The best hardware and software for your company are those which satisfy the requirements of your new business processes. This is what provides competitive differentiation and advantage. We are not suggesting clone organizations.

Because stand-alone systems do not allow for integration and because the new business paradigm is based on collaboration and integration, transferring data among organizations and with consumers is critical for success. One prediction is

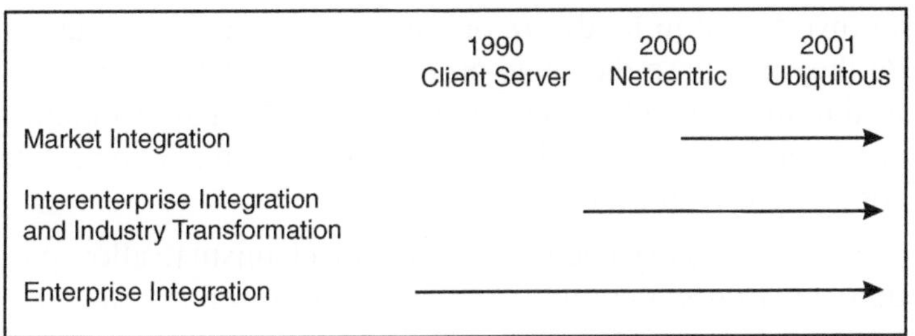

FIGURE 7.2. Technology Vision 2000+ (*Source:* Glaser, Peter [2000], Presentation at Anderson Consulting Chicago Office [July].)

that more information will be coming in the next two years than in the past 10,000.[10] New servers and storage capability will be necessary to handle the increase in information. Sharing data efficiently can happen only if core technologies and standards are unified.

CORE TECHNOLOGIES AND STANDARDS

Without a standardized system, every manufacturer would be free to create its own format for codes. In this scenario, Xerox might establish one code for printers, Hewlett-Packard could create another, and Lexmark could create another, resulting in increased inefficiency, duplication, and escalating hardware expenses. To avoid this scenario, companies in several industries voluntarily agreed to have the Uniform Code Council (UCC) create a symbology system for Uniform Product Classification (UPC) codes. The UCC assigns the the numbers to be used to identify manufacturer products, sizes, colors, and case markings. In addition to the ability to identify what is being sold, in what quantities, and to whom, the UCC system makes collaboration possible because data can be shared between trading partners.

> "If they [standards] aren't created, there will be 5,000 ways to do something, and we'll still have to communicate with the rivet guy who uses a fax machine."
>
> Johnson Controls, Internetweek.com, Sept. 17, 2001

While standards exist or are being created for basic classification (bar codes or transmission of ordering data), companies do not necessarily use the same hardware or software to capture and analyze the information. Not all companies make

"We believe participating [in an exchange] will enable Kroger and others to achieve a richer data exchange at a lower transaction cost."

Gary Rhodes, The Kroger Co., *Supermarket News,* April 2, 2001

"It's challenging to figure out a way to integrate transactions from the website with the flow of transactions through your ERP system so they are aggregated into the production planning."

Jeff Morgan, CIO and Vice President of Information Technology, *Consumer Goods Technology,* Sept. 2000

an investment in hardware or software at the same time nor do they purchase the same product brands. They cannot afford to immediately change the way their data are formatted or to purchase new hardware or software to make their data compatible with every trading partner.

Exchanges have been created as a mechanism to allow participants to use a common platform for presenting information to partners and to share information among themselves. In the grocery and CPGs industry, several exchanges have emerged, such as GlobalNetExchange (GNX), World Wide Retail Exchange (WWRE), Transora.com, CPGmarket.com, and RetailersMarketXchange, Inc. In the transporation industry, 100 to 150 exchanges exist.[11]

UCC is perceived as a neutral, trusted nonprofit organization. Building on this reputation, UCCnet was established to facilitate interoperability by providing product registry services, enabling synchronization of item and location information among trading partners, trade exchanges, and national data pools.[12] As a neutral playing field, UCCnet will ensure that data are standards compliant and facilitate interoperability in a secure environment.

Kraft and Shaw's were the first manufacturer and retailer team to be production certified by UCCnet.[13] They completed the certification process by sending and receiving Extensible Markup Language (XML) data through UCCnet for fifteen business processes. Using UCCnet services, Kraft and Shaw's are able to reduce errors and decrease lead time requirements for new product introductions and changes to item information. They also have a synchronized product authorization file to ensure the right information for the right products is always available to both organizations. Shaw's subscribes to receive information on Kraft products that it currently sells, or on a Kraft product that it might be interested in selling. When Kraft updates product information or introduces a new item, the information is communicated to Shaw's via UCCnet. Companies find that participating in an exchange provides a more cost-effective alternative for exchanging data and that it is more efficient to use the Internet for exchanging information.

Until recently, there was no system of worldwide product codes or standards for electronic data interchange. Because of the confusion resulting from multiple production descriptions and bar codes, multiple EDI standards for simple processes like ordering and paying, multiple intelligent tagging standards, multiple XML standards, and multiple efficient consumer response scorecards, the Global Commerce Initiative (GCI) was established in July 1999. The group includes about twenty multinational retailers and their suppliers, thirty-six Efficient Consumer Response (ECR) groups around the world, and the major standard-setting organizations, i.e., European Article Numbering (EAN) International, Uniform Code Council (UCC), Comité Européen de Normalisation (CEN) or European Committee for Standardization, International Standards Organization (ISO), Voluntary Interindustry Commerce Standards (VICS), Center for International Economic Studies (CIES), Food Marketing Institute (FMI), the Association for Automatic Identification (AIM) and Data Capture Technologies, and the Grocery Manufacturers of America (GMA).

"[L]ess than 2% of the company's 5,000 active suppliers communicate with the contract manufacturers using EDI. And while penetration is somewhat higher in certain pockets—like the automotive vertical system—it is clear that the adoption of EDI as a mainstream communication vehicle will not happen."

Steve Geary, Vice President of Product Management, Tilion, *World Trade,* August 2001

The purpose of the GCI is to improve the performance of the international supply chain for CGCs and retailers through the collaborative endorsement of recommended standards. The participants are organized into four working groups: Product Identification, Intelligent Tagging, Global Scorecard, and Business Process Group.[14] As a result of this initiative, standards for XML, an Extensible Markup Language used for defining data elements on Web pages and on business-to-business documents were released on July 1, 2001. GCI is not a standards body but is a group of global users who are working to facilitate the identification and adoption of global standards across a number of industries. For example, major travel industry players, including airlines, car rental companies, travel agencies, and hotel chains, released final versions of industry-specific standards. The Open Travel Alliance proposed these standards to enable companies to conduct electronic transactions more efficiently.[15]

"If you look back in history, the grocery industry has been first in adapting things like the UPC. . . . So the grocery industry will be among the first to embrace XML standards."

Terry Erman, Director of Marketing and Public Relations, UCC, *Supermarket News,* June 11, 2001

As more companies and people around the world use the Internet for exchanging information, data format is only one aspect of standardization to be considered. In 1988, seven countries were connected to the Internet; 214 countries were connected in 2000. Almost a third of the people in developed countries have access to the Internet.[16] While the percentage of computers per household in developing countries is very low, many people still have access to the Internet by visiting Internet cafés or using cell phones or personal digital assistants. Internet usage by such a wide audience does pose some challenges. Today, 52.4 percent of the world's online population does not speak English. Predictions are that by 2003 U.S. citizens will comprise only a third of the online population, that 66 percent of e-commerce spending will originate from outside the United States, that Chinese will be the most widely used language on the Internet by 2007, that by 2002 most Internet users will have a mother tongue other than English, and that by 2003 a third of Web users will be using another language online.[17] With so many people outside the United States using the Internet, language must also be considered a standardization issue.

"If I'm selling to you, I speak your language. If I'm buying, dann mussen Sie Deutsch sprechen [then you must speak German]."

Willy Brandt, Former Chancellor of Germany

The lack of a common language and common culture results in a lack of standardization, thereby presenting another hurdle for collaboration. Web sites need to be multilingual so that consumers can understand the information being presented. Translation software is available for translating Web site display information; it also enables consumer inquiries and company responses to be translated into the the user's language. That software is not perfect yet; it is still being refined. At the same time, some global vendors are trying to create software for terminology management, project management, and multilingual content management. However, recognizing that a standardized language does not exist means that a method for communicating effectively on the Internet must be established.

"Clearly achieving globalization is not as simple as clicking a button. But when the world starts voting with its money, both software vendors and traditional brick-and-mortar companies will have to take a global view in order to succeed."

Dennis Bartlar, "Global Village," www.line56.com, August 15, 2001

One estimate is that international markets will account for 40 percent of the total e-commerce by 2003. Idiom Technologies estimates that Internet use is expected to grow 79 percent in Asia, 123 percent in Latin America, and 2,000 percent in Japan over the next few years. With this type of global growth, worldwide standards for data, processes, and exchange of information are critical for collaboration.

BUSINESS APPLICATIONS

If standards, technologies, hardware, and processes are in place that allow for accurate and timely exchanges of data, then the data can be used to implement strategies. Not all hardware works efficiently to accomplish all tasks. Not all software performs all required activities. Not all software and hardware are compatible. So, you need to make wise choices.

Where can you begin? You must begin with your company's mission statement. How are you trying to position your organization in the community, with your employees, with your shareholders, with consumers, and with your suppliers? With whom do you want to collaborate? What kind of collaboration do you want? How do consumers come in contact with your company? What data need to be made available to which employees to enable them to communicate effectively with consumers? Which department needs what information?

"You have to assess what your market strategy is, and only then can you really decide what technologies you should use to integrate the different parts of your business."

Dan Focazio, Vice President of e-business, Acuent, *Consumer Goods Technology,* Sept. 2000

First, you need to know what products consumers want at what price as well as how consumers prefer to make their purchases and have them delivered. Second, you need to know who the business partners are with whom you will be collaborating, what strategies your organization plans to accomplish, and what strategies your business partner would like to accomplish. Third, you need to reengineer your organization and business processes to accomplish your goals.

Changing business processes with clear objectives in mind is critical for success. With a variety of hardware and software systems available, companies can choose a software system and let it dictate business processes. However, hardware and software are really tools—not all tools work well for the same job. You need to choose the tools that work well for the job you have in mind. Of course there will always be

"You have to recognize that tools are just tools, but they do have an impact when they are used as part of a major corporate effort."

Darrell Rigby, Director, Bain and Company, June 13, 2001

unintended consequences requiring additional modification. However, you want to choose the software or hardware that best accomplishes goals that are consistent with your mission. For example, Microsoft installed an internal purchasing system that was used by 11,000 Microsoft employees per month. It cut the cost of sending purchase orders to vendors by $43 per transaction, resulting in a 72 percent reduction in cost.[18] However, investment in technology does not always have such a positive ROI.

Mott's, for example, planned to improve in-stock customer service while reducing inventory. To accomplish that goal, they chose software that required going beyond their legacy business systems into the world of e-enabled systems.[19] This meant using a third party to host its Web site and converting all Web orders into Mott's existing EDI format so the data could then be transmitted into Mott's enterprise database system. The next major step was upgrading demand planning processes. Jeff Morgan, CIO, commented, "The project never ends. It is a constant drive forward."

"It's very easy to fall into the trap where you look for silver-bullet solutions to improve customer relations and increase customer retention."

Ray McKenzie, DMR Consulting, informationweek.com, July 13, 2001

Since meeting consumers' needs is the central principle of this new collaborative business paradigm, Customer Relationship Management (CRM) software is extremely popular. It is a $6.5 billion software industry enabling companies to understand and anticipate the needs of their current and potential customer base. Everyone, from sales, operations, management, customer support, and even the customer, needs access to this information. This is a major long-term investment of time and money. It can take years to fully implement and cost millions of dollars. First, the data gathered by your company from all departments need to be "clean"—checked for accuracy and formatted appropriately. Second, connecting a call center, a Web site, and a database with one another is a complex task.[20] Third, costs for training, networking, customization, and integration can easily cost up to four times the price of the software itself. Some estimates suggest that a comprehensive CRM project could cost up to $5 million.[21]

In many cases, CRM software was presented in an overly simplified fashion, leading companies to believe that they could install off-the-counter software to achieve customized results. One estimate is that 19 percent of users defected from using CRM solutions. It is not plug-and-play software. Rather, implementation of CRM requires careful analysis and planning to determine which software and hardware will enable the company to accomplish its mission and how the hardware will be integrated into the newly designed business processes.

Employees' roles and responsibilities need to be redefined and information needs to be shared internally in new ways. The system needs to allow consumers to interact with the company in the format they choose: by phone, by fax, in person, or via the Internet. In addition, consumers should be able to find answers to questions by themselves and place orders in a manner convenient to them. The CRM system also needs to be sensitive to the needs of your business partners. For instance, are retailers likely to have a problem with your Web site if consumers can purchase from you over the Web rather than in their stores or on their Web sites? By exchanging information with trading partners, inventory, delivery, and assortment decisions can be coordinated based upon consumer purchases. By mining the data in your system, you can target prospects in a more cost-efficient manner. If planning and reengineering of business processes is done well, if the best hardware and software are purchased, and if standards and exchanges are used to ensure data compatibility, then the use of CRM software can have a dramatic effect.

"If you don't have a good customer-facing process and you automate it, then you've just automated the problem."

Barton Goldenberg, Information Systems Marketing, informationweek.com, July 13, 2001

Nygard International is a textile company that collects data every night from 200 stores serving over 300,000 customers and pulls the data into its central data warehouse. Once a week, Nygard gets point of sale information from major accounts via EDI transaction.[22] Marketing uses the data to determine the design of next year's fashions. Merchandising uses the data to determine what is selling in the stores. Notices are sent to consumers when new lines of items they have purchased in the past come into the store. The information on consumer sales allows the retailers to know their con-

"We've always said we were on a journey. We don't know where the end is, and we are willing to invest and change and invest and change."

Patrick Steele, Vice President, Information Systems and Technology, Albertson's, *Supermarket News,* April 2, 2001

sumers better, to respond to consumers' preferences, to communicate more effectively with them, and to manage the production process more efficiently. The next step on Nygard's journey is to determine a more efficient way of getting the information back to retailers who are all asking for the information to be laid out in a different format.

In another example, P&G began with a business problem—a high rate of out-of-stock merchandise. Lost sales could be measured in the billions of dollars. First, a sophisticated algorithm for point-of-sale item scans was created to detect out-of-stocks or unusually slow-moving items. A monitor was created to detect anomalies and send a message to a designated store manager or retail floor employee. The problem is not solved, however, until someone does something about it. Pilot tests for improving this business process are in progress. This particular project reflects a change in how managers at P&G approach technology. Rather than identifying an application for technology, managers began searching for technology to help solve a business problem.[23]

Technology exists to accomplish almost any integrative, collaborative task. Many different types of technology exist. You need to decide what goals you are trying to accomplish and then search for the hardware and software that are most consistent with your business mission and that can be used collaboratively with your business partners on the tasks you jointly choose.

Bain and Company conducts a yearly survey to determine what software business executives find most useful for what tasks. The most recent results are in Box 7.1.[24] One piece of technology does not work in all situations. If you don't know where you are going, any piece of hardware or software will work or fail equally well. If you know where you are going, you can choose the best tool for the job. The right tool is only successful if people are able to use it well. The business change process is 80 percent people and only 20 percent technology. The people part relates to the culture, the education process, the training, and the retraining.

BOX 7.1. Bain and Company Survey Results

- Best for financial results:

  Cycle-time reduction
  Pay-for-performance
  Strategic planning
- Best for growing customer equity:

  Customer satisfaction measurement
  Total quality management
  Customer relationship marketing
  One-to-one marketing
- Best for improving competitive positioning:

  Strategic planning
  Strategic alliances
  Customer satisfaction measurement
- Best for long-term performance capabilities:

  Strategy planning
  Cycle-time reduction
  Growth strategies
- Best for bolstering integration efforts across the organization:

  Strategic planning
  Balanced scorecard
  Mission and vision statements

Source: Adapted from Rigby, Darrell, "Tried and True Beats Out New Economy Tools by 2:1" (2001), Bain and Company's 8th Annual "Management Tools" survey, <bain.com> (June 13).

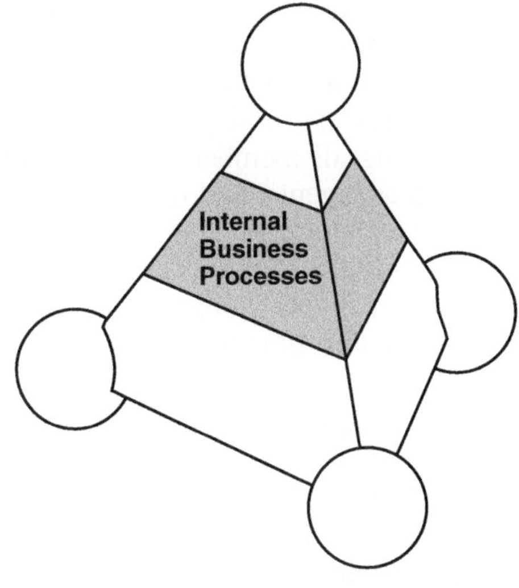

Chapter 8

Internal Business Processes

"Most ailing organizations have developed a functional blindness to their own defects. They are not suffering because they cannot resolve their problems but because they cannot see their problems."

John Gardner

Today's business environment presents an ever-changing set of demands. Knowing **your** end consumers' current needs, purchasing habits, and decision-making processes is critical for success. The mass market of consumers no longer exists. In its place are multidimensional consumers—the same person belongs to different groups of consumers depending upon the product, service, or circumstance. These multidimensional consumers are also multichannel consumers, meaning that they contact your company with whatever channel of communication is convenient to them at the moment: in person, phone, fax, mail, or Internet. They expect seamless service regardless of the channel used. The demand side of the business environment has changed forever.

At the same time, every company is under tremendous pressure to increase efficiencies and cut costs. New product development costs must be trimmed. The goal of this new business paradigm is for production to be driven by consumer purchases, necessitating the timely and accurate exchange of information among all members of the channel. Standards, exchange services, agents, and new software facilitate this process. Using technology collaboratively to address supply chain issues is critical for success. The supply side of the business environment has changed forever. There is no longer room for inefficient practices that do not add VALUE.

"Going beyond ERP, really is, as noted, a total exercise of realigning strategies and structures and systems and skills to match the marketplace and its demands."

Angeline Pantages, Managing Editor, *Consumer Goods Technology,* Jan./Feb. 2000

This new collaborative business paradigm that strives to serve consumer needs is challenging and not easily adopted. It is **NOT** a project. It will **NOT** be successfully implemented by one department in your organization. It requires visible commitment by top management to a change in business processes. Identifying the new strategic direction of a company is the first step; getting all the employees (whether that number is ten or 200,000) to change their everyday practices to achieve that objective is more difficult. This chapter will examine six factors that are based on an organizational performance model created by Dave Hanna, author of *Designing Organizations for High Performance*. These six factors are interdependent, are the part of the process that determines how people in an organization behave on a daily basis, and determine how well daily business practices in a company work to implement the business strategy:[1] Structure, Tasks, People, Information, Decision Making, and Rewards.

STRUCTURE

This new business paradigm has a heavy information requirement, demanding data about consumers, suppliers, logistics, invoices, payment, cash flow, and cost of activities. Having the right structure means having the right people linked together to work on the right tasks. For instance, a traditional buyer-seller relationship works in a confrontational, adversarial relationship or a transactional buying situation (see Figure 8.1). Coordination of activities and information takes place internally and then the buyer and seller communicate each organization's position and negotiate an agreement, using other departments and functions as resources on an "as needed" basis.

The business processes employed in the new business process paradigm require cross-functional information sharing, decision making, and planning within an organization (see Figure 8.2). Collaborative business activities require new ways of working between organizations and that topic will be addressed in the next chapter. This discussion focuses on the way the internal structure of a company needs to change to facilitate cross-functional activities. The specific functions involved depend upon the company, the task, and the trading partner.

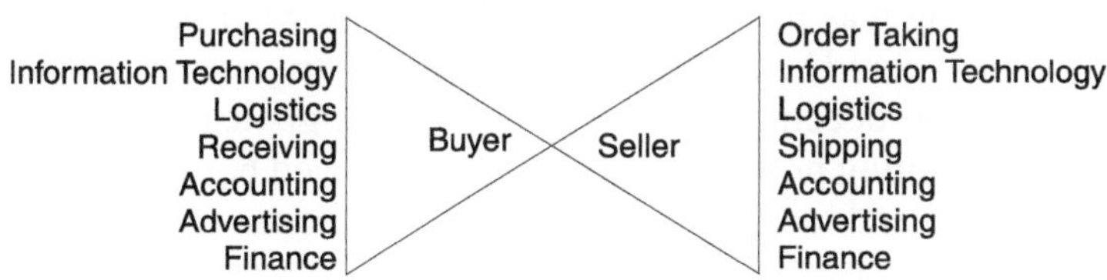

FIGURE 8.1. Traditional Buyer-Seller Relationship

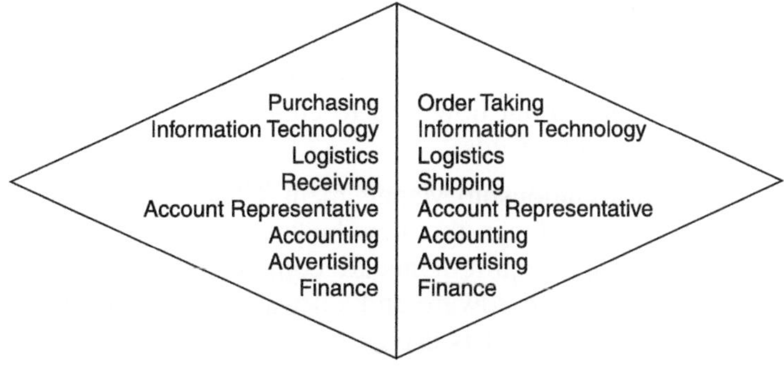

FIGURE 8.2. Collaborative Relationships

The Kroger Co. found that to facilitate the change process within their company, the functional areas of accounting, human resources, information systems, purchasing, and distribution needed representation.[2] Since change included the use of new technology, information systems people needed to be included in the discussions from the very beginning, so they could identify what was feasible and understand what the process was trying to accomplish before designing or changing information technology requirements. The more they understood what the group wanted, the easier it was to find appropriate solutions. New technologies and new activities required specifying skills, selecting the people who had relevant skills, and developing appropriate training programs. Therefore, the human resource department played an important role.

In the decision to coordinate some procurement processes, purchasing was involved to help determine what purchasing decisions could be coordinated without destroying the autonomy of the decentralized structure. The logistical decisions of determining how products would be moved between manufacturers and local stores required the presence of representatives from distribution. The accounting representatives helped determine not just which alternatives provided the lowest cost but also which activities and alternatives provided the best value. Traditionally, each of these departments made its own decisions on what business practices and behaviors should be implemented. Using this new collaborative business paradigm, the cross-functional group exchanged information, discussed issues from a variety of perspectives, and made decisions about how best to create efficiencies while meeting consumer needs.

Customer Relationship Management (CRM) strategies and software are popular in this new business paradigm. While the technological requirements are complex, requiring difficult integration of hardware and software, less than 10 percent of a CRM project is driven by technology.[3] Managers must not go through the implementation process quickly without taking time to win top management and employee user support or the business processes will not be changed to correspond with the project goals.

The Regence Group, a holding company for four Blue Cross Blue Shield operations in Idaho, Oregon, Utah, and Washington, created a group of underwriters, customer service personnel, members of the information technology staff, and business managers to deploy a unified CRM strategy.[4] To be successful, the group had to have senior management endorsement and user buy-in. The group worked for six months determining the business requirements for the system. Sales teams had to be realigned and training was necessary, taking even more time; once implemented, 85 percent of the users found the new system to be valuable. Since the initial expectation was that there would be a 50/50 split in terms of support, the 85 percent endorsement was very positive. Nine people from all areas of the operations continue to be part of this group to discuss improvements. Within the first several months, the group had already found areas for improvement. Because the business environment and consumers are not static, this cross-functional approach to changing business processes is a journey and not an end point.

Rosalie Duong at Qiagen, a biotechnology company, took a long route to get implementation of CRM within the company.[5] First, a single user group was created consisting of business, technology, and top sales personnel. This group identified thirty key requirements that the new process would have to accomplish. Second, a survey was sent to all 300 members of the global sales force asking for their input on what was necessary to make the proposed process work effectively. After sending e-mail reminders, all 300 surveys were returned. Third, the Single User Group prioritized the requirements and presented them to six CRM software vendors before choosing a software vendor. The CRM software chosen did fit the user requirements and has been implemented successfully.

Today's organizational structures typically function in silos of responsibility, measuring and rewarding individuals and departments, not teams. To be successful in this new business paradigm, the structure of organizations needs to facilitate cross-functional work and decision making. Having people from different functional departments work together is not easy—their perspectives are different, their work goals as well as their measurements and rewards can be different, their styles are often different. Learning to work toward a common goal may take some time and may even involve performing new tasks, and changing measurements and rewards.

TASKS

Trainers are fond of saying that you should "work smarter, not harder." What kinds of tasks are required in this new collaborative, consumer-centric business environment? What do you need to do to work smarter?

In an environment in which data are transmitted between companies electronically and many of the ordering decisions are transmitted electronically, what are the roles of the buyer and seller in today's marketplace? Securing a repeat order is not the primary goal. Many organizations have changed the name of their salespeople to Customer Business Development Representatives. With orders being placed and filled electronically, the buyer and seller no longer need to discuss when and what should be purchased under ordinary circumstances. The roles of the buyer and seller are now strategic: How should orders be changed in extraordinary circumstances? When are new products being introduced? How should they be introduced? How should new consumer insights be used? How can new consumers be attracted? What data are available and how can they be used to add **value?** Now, discussions are more oriented toward what can be done to grow the business rather than what quantity of product should be ordered at what price.

"The mistake some companies make is they deploy the software and expect it to take care of itself."

Scott DeNies, Manager of Interplan Market Strategy, Regence, July 13, 2001

When implementing this new business paradigm, organizations create new cross-functional and collaborative structures; these structures also entail new tasks. Identifying and defining the new tasks is one part of the process. Enabling and empowering people to perform new tasks is another challenge.

PEOPLE

Identifying and developing skills of existing employees, hiring new employees with relevant skills, and training employees to perform new tasks are all critical for success. First, the company needs to specify the required skills, identify the people within the organization who have the required skills, or hire people with the required skills. Second, employees need to know what behaviors are required in their new jobs. Third, training is required so employees become familiar with using the new tools and techniques and feel comfortable working within the new structure.

"Technology changes rapidly; people do not."

David Wessell, *The Wall Street Journal,* Feb. 15, 2001

When Shell Energy first installed LodeStar's billing and forecasting application for the energy industry, employees did not use it. While the software was available, the employees continued to do the billing process by hand because they did not feel comfortable relying on the accuracy of the software. Shell created training programs. After several months, the employees became comfortable with the software and no longer resorted to doing everything by hand.[6] Then, the billing process went from taking six to seven hours every night to two hours a night.

The process of adopting new business processes at the Kroger Co. necessitated a great deal of training. Many of the top executives and store managers attended seminars on cash flow, category management, and activity-based costing. The training programs addressed several questions: What is this new business process? How do the new processes affect my job? How does ROI relate to my job? How are the activities and processes measured? What new behaviors do I have to perform? What are the new behaviors I need to explain to my employees? The Kroger Co. developed its own Category Management University and employees continue to be involved in many hours of training programs.

Eagles Flight Creative Training Excellence, Inc., encountered problems when adding CRM software to its call center.[7] First, employees in the call center who were going to be using the software were not involved in the decision to purchase the Siebel package. Second, no one explained the benefits of using the new software to the employees. As a result, the employees saw it as just more work—entering more information in more fields. They complained about the software and were not happy about using it. Eagles Flight has had to backtrack and begin training programs in an attempt to explain the benefits of using the software. However, the company is now making those presentations to a defensive audience. The time required to gain acceptance will be doubled or tripled when having to perform those steps after employees have already developed a negative attitude about the process, software, or new tasks. Companies must determine what processes allow people to have access to accurate information on a timely basis.

INFORMATION

In this new business environment, requirements for information have escalated dramatically. However, providing every employee with every piece of data would result in information overload. Companies need to design processes so that people receive or have access to accurate and timely information when it is needed to perform their tasks and make decisions.

"You'll never make dramatic progress unless you engineer around legacy systems and legacy people."

Robert J. Herbold, Executive Vice President, Microsoft, *Supermarket News,* April 2, 2001

For example, brand managers, marketers, and sales managers all need access to consumer data. They may want the information in the same formats; they may want the information in different formats. Their analyses may require information from accounting, shipping, an outside marketing research firm, one of the exchanges, or a distributor. Gathering the data from separate locations is one challenge; making the data from separate files compatible so analyses can be performed is another challenge; presenting the data in different formats is yet another challenge.

Many companies have found the Internet to be of great service in making data accessible to many people in a variety of locations on a real-time basis. Data can be stored on a particular Web site; access is possible from a variety of locations; access can be protected by password codes. The balance among flexibility, easy access, and security makes the Internet a preferred choice for many companies.

Johnson & Johnson created a Web site for small retailers carrying Johnson & Johnson products.[8] One part of the Web site provides small retailers with access to a self-service method for placing orders, checking order status, and reviewing their accounts. These customers enjoy having immediate access to information and getting their questions answered promptly.

Technology, if chosen with specific objectives, company requirements, and consumer needs in mind, makes it possible to provide all parties with the information they need, when they need it, in a secure environment.

DECISION MAKING

When companies use new structures and business processes and have employees performing new tasks, the traditional decision-making processes may no longer work well. In general, companies need to manage risk and generate a profit by balancing the need to meet consumers' needs and cut costs.

The traditional methods of allocating overhead costs to make decisions are out of date and current financial reporting does not reflect operational changes. In today's new business paradigm, gross margin analyses do **NOT** necessarily lead to profitable decisions. To be useful, allocation of overhead costs needs to be accurate. Activity Based Costing (ABC) is a methodology that measures the cost and performance of activities in a way that recognizes the cause and effect relationships of cost drivers to activities.[9]

"Wal-Mart sells 63% of its inventory before it must pay for the goods . . . and expects to turn all of its inventory before bills come due in about three years' time."

Supermarket News, Nov. 22, 1999

ABC is **NOT** accounting (debits and credits). ABC does **NOT** use a traditional costing approach that allocates costs based upon volume or product cost. ABC does **NOT** assume that costs vary with volume. ABC does **NOT** allocate costs based on an arbitrary percentage. ABC **IS** knowing what money is assigned to what activity and what drives that activity. ABC **IS** assigning costs based on how resources and activities are consumed. ABC **DOES** assume that activities consume costs and that processes consume different levels of activities.

For example, assume your store sells 1,000,000 sweaters annually at the price of $15.00 (see Table 8.1). If only acquisition and sales costs are used to determine gross margin, the decision that makes sense is to go with Option One. However, the sweaters in Option One are delivered lying flat in boxes and have to be placed on hangers. The sweaters in Option Two are delivered on hangers. When including the cost of the activity of putting the sweaters on hangers, the profitable decision is to go with Option Two. Knowing the costs of all activities related to acquiring **and** selling a product or service is necessary to make profitable decisions.

What happens when you change business processes? What are the activities involved in the process? How much does each activity cost? ABC assigns costs to specific activities. By doing that, you can identify which activities drive the cost of a specific business process. For instance, The Kroger Co. identified thirty-two major activities in their supply chain (see Figure 8.3). The result of their analysis was that 44 percent of Kroger's cost was associated with receiving the product. The next task was to explore the costs, and especially cost savings, of implementing alternative processes. For instance, The Kroger Co. normally received eight pallets of

TABLE 8.1. Hypothetical Example

Option One	**Option Two**
Sales Price: $15.00	Sales Price: $15.00
Acquisition Cost: $10.00	Acquisition Cost: $10.15
Gross Margin: 33%	Gross Margin: 32%
Internal Cost to Apply Hanger: $.25	
Total Cost: $10.25	Total Cost: $10.15
Net Profitability: $4.75	Net Profitability: $4.85
1,000,000 × .10 = $100,000 less profit	

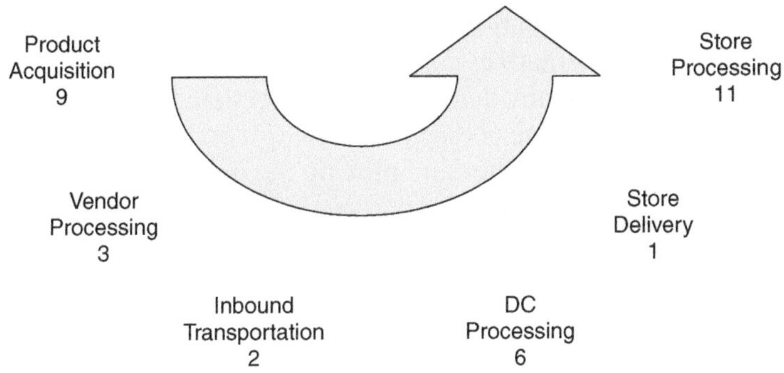

FIGURE 8.3. ABC at Kroger* (*Source:* Cleve Gorman [1997] and Mike Purdum [2002]. Presentations at Xavier University for MBA Class. *Numbers represent number of activities.)

Coke and entered the data into the computer while the Coca-Cola driver stocked them on the shelf. It took thirty minutes of time for a clerk to receive the product and get it into the system. Entering data into the computer when the order is placed made it possible to create the bill of lading, shipping documents, and prepare invoices without having anyone re-key the data into a computer. If the Coke driver is able to come into the store, stage the product, and put it on the shelf without retailer involvement, it would take out about $5 million of costs.

The object is to be able to determine the cost of the activities in the process. What does it cost for cases of candy to get through the distribution center? What does it cost to handle a special order? However, identifying the cost drivers of a specific activity is only one advantage. ABC also allows for making "what-if" assessments.

For example, what if aisle-ready pallets, which were able to go directly from the truck to the aisle in a store, were prepared at the distribution center? The process does add cost in the distribution center and you are able to determine that cost. Does the process also take cost out of the backroom process of receiving, storing, and putting product out in the aisle? If we take more cost out of the backroom process than the cost added at the distribution center, then that alternative makes sense. Other alternatives can also be evaluated. "What if" the distribution company delivers the product to the store? Is that a more cost-effective choice than having a company truck go to the distribution center and pick up the product?

With the tool of ABC, you can identify all the activities in a process, identify the cost of each activity, and identify which activities drive the cost of the process. While ABC provides data regarding alternative choices, those data do not necessarily determine the decision. Sometimes spending money on a more expensive activity is a good decision because that activity attracts your most profitable consumers. Sometimes the more expensive activity enables you to test consumer response or attract new consumers. Experience and business strategies, as well as ABC data, all need to be used when making decisions about which business processes will be used.

ABC, as a tool, provides useful cost information. However, cost is not the only criterion in making business decisions. Data on cost **AND** your intuitive understanding of your market and consumers are necessary for managing risk and generating profit.This process is referred to as Activity Based Management (ABM).

REWARDS

"All organizations are perfectly designed to get the results they get."

Dave Hanna, *Designing Organizations for High Performance,* 1988

The structure is modified, the tasks are defined, the costs are identified, the people are chosen, the training is complete, now what happens? Do the employees perform the new tasks? Do the new processes work? Only if desired behaviors are measured and rewarded, and undesired behaviors are discouraged. For example, salespeople will not engage in cross-selling if they get paid based upon only what their own department sells.

Employees will perform the activities for which they are rewarded. Therefore, you need a system that will measure and reward appropriate activities. A number of measurement tools and metrics can be used:[10]

- Financial
  Profit and loss measures, e.g., contribution to margin
  Return on investment
- Inventory
  Turnover
  Inventory levels
  Stock to sales ratios
  Markdown dollars/liquidation loss
  ROII (Return on Inventory Invested)
- Forecast Accuracy
  Sales forecast accuracy
  Order forecast accuracy
  Frequency of emergency or canceled orders
  Collaborative planning and forecasting replenishment
- "Perfect Order"
  Percent delivered on time
  Percent delivered as ordered
  Percent delivered undamaged
  Percent of orders complete
- Customer Service
  In-stock percent at point of sale
  Purchase order fill rate percent
  Lost sales analysis
  Cycle time
  Customer satisfaction
  Yield
  Reliability

Not all tools are relevant in a particular situation. Not all tools will provide useful information. Choose the best measurement tool based upon your objectives. For instance, if you focus on cash flow, dollars are a more effective measure than margin percentages.

Measuring employees' activities is an important part of the process of changing behavior in the organization. Rewards need to be tied to desired behavior. In the case of Fleming, in which eighty account executives were trained to be long-term strategic facilitators, their bonuses were changed to be tied to the success of their accounts in meeting their sales and profit goals. BPDirect wanted customers and sales representatives to use a new system for improving sales and cutting costs. They offered free fuel cards for Amoco and BP stations for customers and sales staff who used the system. The cards were distributed, however, only once the salespeople were able to get customers registered on the Web site.

Besides rewarding positive behavior, another option is to discourage undesired behavior. For example, Dain Rauscher Wessels, Inc., a New York financial services company, tied employee compensation to their use of CRM software.[11] First, the sales representatives and research analysts were trained to gather data through the CRM system and send messages and customer data using Blackberry (wireless e-mail pager) accounts. Employee use of the application was monitored. Sales representatives did not receive commissions for any sales that were not entered into the new CRM system, thereby discouraging continued use of the old system. Studies, data, and information do not get most people to change. Rather, employees generally perform activities that are measured and directly tied to rewards. They ask and respond to the question, "What's in it for me?"

Today's dynamic business environment demands a change from traditional business processes. Creating an organization that performs cross-functional activities in collaboration with partners to create products and services that can be delivered to consumers in an efficient manner is a major paradigm change. Changing internal business processes is a major challenge.

The impediments are many: human and financial resource commitments, senior management commitment, culture change, modification of organizational structure, creation of new measurements, rewards/incentives tied to new behaviors, and understanding consumer buying habits. Changes need to be consistent with the organization's mission and objectives. Addressing consumer needs must be an important goal for all business decisions. Overcoming impediments and implementing organizational change requires attention to all six of the interrelated elements related to organizational change—structure, tasks, people, information, decision making, and rewards. Each organization will develop a unique solution addressing these six factors and implementing processes that meet its goals.

"Many businesses implement software and hope everything will go well. Or they come up with a five-year CRM deployment plan and three years from now forget what the goals were."

Ray McKenzie,
DMR Consulting,
informationweek.com,
July 13, 2001

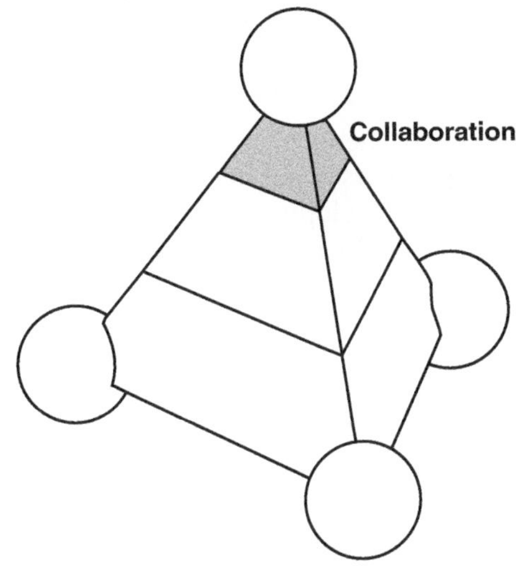

Chapter 9

Collaboration

"Collaboration is about employees from different parts of the enterprise, your business partners and even customers, all working together on an integrated system to improve an organization's relationships with its customers."

Jenny Belser
Senior Consultant, Peppers and Rogers Group
1to1 Magazine, October 2001

Sharing information across functions as well as incorporating consumer data stored within the organization or gathered by outside organizations provides a well-rounded database of information that can be accessed when creating products and services or developing other marketing strategies. Advances in technology make it possible for everyone in the organization to have access to the data they need when they need it. Coordinating internal business processes is essential for success in this new business paradigm. However, the successful companies motoring down the superhighway

"A true partnership is when a supplier helps us advance into new processes."

Michael Terpkosh,
Corporate Director,
Supervalu,
Progressive Grocer,
Dec. 1988

do not operate in isolation. The best efficiencies occur when partners work together in Win-Win-Win-Win* situations. As an advertisement by J. D. Edwards in *The Wall Street Journal* on May 17, 2000 stated, **"Collaborate or Die."**

"CRM projects that don't integrate customer touch points are destined for abject failure."

Liz Shahnam, Meta Group, *Business Week,* July 3, 2000

Since consumers control where, when, and under what format they will purchase products or services, companies must internally organize around developing a seamless process of information sharing between the front and back offices so all employees who come in contact with consumers (consumer touch points) can operate consistently. Therefore, the first section of this chapter addresses Customer Relationship Management (CRM). The second section of this chapter examines the process of collaboration: how to begin, issues to consider, and tools. The third section addresses barriers to success and **benefits** of adopting collaborative business processes.

CUSTOMER RELATIONSHIP MANAGEMENT

"CRM is fundamentally the expression of the consumer-centric business philosophy. It's how you respond to the fact that customers are now the drivers in our economy."

Dick Lee, High-Yield Marketing, *Business Week,* July 3, 2000

CRM is a "banner" term that includes numerous technologies. Initially CRM was used for sales leads and contact management. In the area of contact management, companies developed ways to present a single face to the consumer across multiple contact points, e.g., call center, Web site, sales representative. Companies soon found they needed systems to record and share information across those contact points so that call center staff members, those receiving messages from the Web site, and sales representatives all had access to the most current consumer information. For instance, Swissotel links all information about their guests obtained from intermediaries, property experiences, and customer profiles. As a result, when a request for a room comes from Ms. Jones, the manager of the hotel in Beijing calls up the file and assigns Ms. Jones a room near the elevator with feather pillows and a Coke when she arrives.[1]

Individualization is important to consumers who can always find another source for the product or service. Accord-

---

*Suppliers, distributors, consumers, shareholders

ing to a study by financial services consulting firm, Speer & Associates, only 2 percent of the 147 financial services providers they polled achieve any level of personalization. A recent study by Peppers and Rogers Group and Roper Starch Worldwide finds impressive benefits for companies that do adopt a relationship strategy. About one-fourth of consumers (26 percent) who rated their primary financial services provider as "poor" on CRM said they were likely to switch away from one or more products during the next twelve months.[2] But only 1 percent of consumers who rated CRM as "high" said they were likely to do so.

"Essentially in the eBusiness economy, you need to deliver customer organizational knowledge on demand, anytime anywhere."

Erin Kinikin, Vice President, Customer Relationship Management, Giga Information Group, *Business Week,* July 3, 2000

A broader notion of CRM includes the identification of a consumer life cycle (presale, postsale, and repurchase) and the determination of a value for consumers.[3] Companies determine how much it costs to generate consumers who are willing to try the product or service, how much it costs to deliver products or services that meet the consumers' needs, and how much it costs to retain loyal consumers. Segmenting consumers by value allows companies to develop cost-effective methods of attracting and retaining consumers in a profitable manner. Not all consumers want or need the same level of contact. By knowing which consumers need what level of contact and what the cost of contacting those consumers is, companies can design appropriate ways of developing proactive business plans.

"In the Internet Economy, you must run well ahead of the competition in the race to satisfy customer demands. You either outperform—adapting with agility, flexibility, and rapid-fire quickness—or you perish. Your best customer is just a mouse click away from a world of competitors."

"How to Thrive in the Internet Economy," *Food Logistics and Retailtech,* Fall 2001

For instance, software is available that will not only identify consumers as they log on but also notify Employee A that Customer X is currently online at the Web site and create a pop-up screen so that Employee A can have online contact with Customer X in real time. If your high value consumers require personalized service and attention and if this kind of personalized attention is appreciated by those high value consumers, investment in this software would be profitable. On the other hand, if your high value consumers prefer phone conversations, software that automatically routes incoming calls to designated customer representatives would be more profitable. In another case, directing low volume consumers to a well-designed Web site would be more cost-effective. The alternative chosen must provide the information consumers want because otherwise they will find a company that does allow them to use their preferred medium of interaction.

Companies need a system that allows them to gather information about consumers and their purchases, a way to segment consumers by value, the processes to provide individualized service to consumers by value. However, ensuring that all your consumers receive the desired product or service when they want it, at a reasonable price, involves coordinating the activities of more than one company. Interdependence is a critical element of this new collaborative business paradigm. Simply put, interdependence recognizes that you cannot go it alone in today's tough, competitive world and you realize that you need one another for SURVIVAL!

PROCESS OF COLLABORATION

Designing products or services, producing them, packaging them, transporting them, promoting them, selling them, getting paid for them, and servicing them involve many organizations. According to Forrester Research, a single global shipment of toys takes an average of twenty-seven parties to get it from point A to point B and 76 percent of logistics managers at major companies cannot monitor products en route.[4] This process involves a number of steps and documents: purchase orders, invoices, promotions, price changes, item maintenance, funds transfer, vendor replenishment, delivery record, payment order, remittance advice, functional acceptance, rejection advice, functional acknowledgement, and advance shipment notice. Collaboration is required to integrate this information because these documents originate in different companies.[5]

"The US Food Marketing Institute said in a 1995 report: 'Today's supply chain consists of a series of individual companies each pushing product to the next player in the supply chain. Each transaction adds substantial costs: selling expense, purchase ordering, order processing, order assembly, shipping, receiving, checking and more.'"

Financial Times, Dec. 1, 1998

To improve efficiencies all along the supply chain, companies employing this new business paradigm are collaborating to integrate product flows from production lines to consumers by using actual demand to drive replenishment. Companies using this paradigm have shifted from just looking at the companies on either side in the chain of parties in the global distribution process to making data available among all relevant partners. Many companies, such as Kmart, Ace Hardware, Best Buy, Canadian Tire, Hewlett-Packard, Kimberly-Clark, Schering-Plough, with suppliers from the textile, chemical, automotive, and technology industries, are using the Internet to develop collaborative processes.[6]

In the past, companies have viewed all other companies as competitors and no information was shared. Keeping information and becoming a gatekeeper was a sign of power. This new business paradigm follows one of Jack Welch's famous sayings, "Share to gain." These collaborative business processes are new kinds of work and can involve activities such as sharing point-of-sale data, or sharing information about consumers, or sharing information about company processes, or sharing information about process improvement and sharing one another's business plans. Deciding what information to share and what information is proprietary is not an easy decision. Creating a collaborative business approach is possible by keeping the focus on the **CONSUMERS.**

"For companies that want to be part of the twenty-first century . . . inventory visibility is essential. They must manage inventory in the entire supply chain from Mother Earth to the ultimate consumer. In an 'e'-enabled world, we'll be able to do that. And companies that don't adopt these new practices? In the food industry, they'll be acquired, in other industries they'll go out of business."

James E. Morehouse, Senior Vice President, AT Kearney, Logistics Supplement, *Consumer Goods Technology,* May 2001

Culture Change

Changing to a collaborative process is a definite culture change with several conditions necessary for success. First, top management must visibly support the endeavor to switch to a collaborative business paradigm. Second, serving the consumers' needs must be the ultimate goal. Third, identifying partners and the form of collaboration must be a choiceful activity. This change in business processes is time-consuming, requires financial and human resources, and involves major organization changes. The biggest cost, however, is the people cost—training, education, and performance measurement.

Choosing a partner with whom to collaborate is an important decision and must be done wisely. Is there a company with whom you have briefly talked about "what if" kinds of activities? Is there a company with whom you share consumers? Is there a company that is interested in pursuing collaborative activities? Is there a company that has expertise and efficiency in an area that needs improvement in your company? Is there a company with which you have a mutual trust? Is

"To optimize the supply chain in the Internet Age, you need near-real-time visibility into the location and movement of goods."

Chris Newton, Senior Analyst, AMR, *Consumer Goods Technology,* May 2001

"In the network model, used by companies like Dell and Amazon.com, 'nobody gets paid until the consumer consumes'."

Patrick Kiernan, President, Dayl Kiernan and Associates, *Food Logistics,* March 2000 there another company that has had success with collaborative activities? Is there an area on which both partners can work and win? By exploring these issues, you can identify a few potential partners and begin exploring the possibility of collaborative activities with them.

Most companies begin with one or a small group of suppliers or customers. In addition, you can begin on a small scale. How can we improve our sales forecasts? How can we increase the efficiency of the delivery process? For instance, a small group of three people from each company might work on a specific project and find a way to cut costs. That success can be highlighted, publicized within the company, and used to build support for moving to a larger, more involved project.

"Collaboration requires more face-to-face interface than there's been before. There's constant feedback that goes on. There's just so much institutional learning to gain about how to work with a trading partner. The technology will catch up. It's best to just get started."

Jack Haedicke, Arena Consulting, *Food Logistics and Retailtech,* Fall 2001

To promote better understanding of shared information when working on joint plans, many organizations have **reorganized** the way they interface with other partner companies. Instead of having the buyer and seller be the contact points between companies, the new approach is that each company creates a team of necessary experts so that people with like backgrounds and expertise can work together on the implementation of a joint plan (see Figure 9.1). The Collaborative Relationships model establishes a link between people from similar functional areas so that the logistics people talk to logistics people, the R&D people talk with R&D people, and information systems people talk with information systems people. This pairing of people with similar perspectives improves the communication and decision process.

The role of the traditional sales representative and buyer changes. As companies develop electronic linkages and orders are generated automatically, the sales representative function changes from obtaining an order to developing joint marketing strategies. All members of the team must learn to think strategically and develop the skills required to work collaboratively with team members from other companies. The Internet is often used as a tool not only for exchanging data but also for monitoring joint plans.

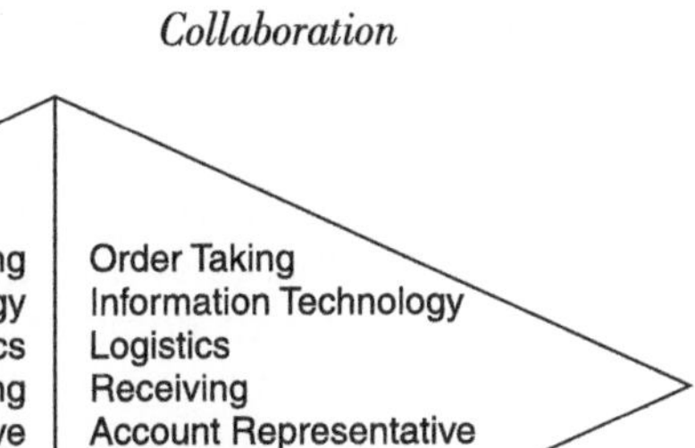

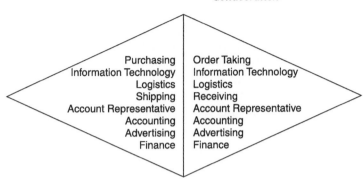

FIGURE 9.1. Collaborative Relationships

This shift is occurring at an ever-accelerating rate. The National Association of Purchasing Management (NAPM) and Forrester Research, Inc., announced that the number of buying organizations that used the Internet to collaborate with suppliers grew to 49.5 percent for the quarter ending in September 2001.[7] Large-volume buyers' collaboration went from 46.4 percent to 63.5 percent and manufacturers' collaboration rose from 40.0 percent to 52.4 percent. These are the companies on the superhighway speeding ahead with increased efficiencies as they provide what consumers want, when they want it, where they chose to buy, and at a fair price.

> "The only thing better than winning is winning together."
>
> Mark Hansen, CEO, Flemming

> "Firms that work together can do so much more than those that work alone. . . . ECR created an industry awareness, but it is not a strategy. Supply chain management reflects a specific strategy."
>
> Don Bowersox, Michigan State University, *Food Logistics,* March 1999

Keeping Score

As the process begins, questions arise involving this new work: What are best practices in this new business paradigm? How far along is my company in terms of implementing best practices? Is my company making progress in a particular area? How do I know if the right opportunities have been identified within my company? How do I know if the right opportunities have been identified with my trading partner? In response to these questions, several **scorecards** have been developed to help in the process of identifying important issues and tracking progress. The Efficient Consumer Response (ECR) group developed a scorecard that was used in the Consumer and Packaged Goods (CPG) industry in the

United States. ECR groups in Europe developed a European Scorecard and ECR groups in Asia developed an Asian Scorecard. Multinational manufacturers and retailers found themselves having to complete three different scorecards; this was not only time-consuming but also created difficulty when comparing results within the company across geographies.

One of the four main areas of activity sponsored by the Global Commerce Initiative (GCI), described in Chapter 8, was to create a Global Scorecard so that concepts and definitions would be standard, thereby facilitating the task of benchmarking. Then, companies would know where they stood in relation to the industry on a particular business activity and they could assess improvement over time. The Global Scorecard involves four Key Components: Demand Management, Supply Management, Enablers, and Integrators (see www.globalscorecard.net). Each of the Key Components encompasses Key Performance Indicators (KPIs) and each of the KPIs has attributes (see Table 9.1). Each of the attributes is scored from zero to four depending upon the level of joint activity being conducted.

To use the scorecard, your company's team would begin by scoring your own company, identifying areas for improvement, and setting priorities of which areas are most important related to your company's mission and goals. The internal implications of changing business processes, such as using activity-based costing metrics or changing reward structures, were addressed in Chapter 8. The team would also go through the scoring process for its partner company, and identify its strengths and areas for improvement. The differences and similarities among companies would be compared. This gap analysis identifies areas that could be improved upon by each organization if all worked together. With this perspective of using collaborative problem solving to provide value to consumers, both parties are ready to meet.

Before conducting a joint session with teams from both companies, a few words of caution are necessary. Preparation includes identifying your company's mission, your partner's

TABLE 9.1. Global Scorecard

ECR Concepts	Key Performance Indicators	Attributes
Demand management	Demand strategy and capabilities	Strategic direction (Consumer value business model)
		Strategic direction (Category management)
	Optimize assortments	Assortment planning
		Assortment execution
		Assortment evaluation
	Optimize promotions	Promotion planning
		Promotion execution
		Promotion evaluation
	Optimize new product introductions (NPI)	NPI planning
		NPI execution
		NPI evaluation
	Consumer value creation	Consumer knowledge management
		Solutions-for-consumers
		Channels-to-consumers
Supply management	Supply strategy and capabilities	Strategic direction
		People and organization
		Information management
	Responsive replenishment	Automated store ordering
		Continuous replenishment
		Product flow techniques
		Transport optimization
		Efficient unit loads
	Integrated demand-driven supply	Synchronized production
		Integrated suppliers
	Operational excellence	Reliable store operations
		Reliable distribution
		Reliable production
Enablers	Common data and communication standards	Product and shipment identification
		Master data alignment
		Electronic data interchange
		Electronic communication standards
	Cost/profit and value measurement	Activity-based costing (ABC)
		Consumer value measurement
Integrators	Collaborative planning	Collaborative planning
	E-business	Business-to-business

mission, common consumers, and areas of potential gain for each side. If only one side has something to gain, the partnership will not work. In preparation for the meeting itself, members need to be instructed that the discussion about scores is **NOT** a personal evaluation about how well individuals are doing their jobs. Rather, it **IS** an evaluation of a company's collaborative activities, so the discussion needs to focus on the company's systems and not on personalities. The scoring process should be done regularly because the most important part of the scoring activity is **NOT** the score but the relative change in the score as joint activities are pursued. During the scoring session, you and your partner will identify a joint project, determine the goals, and specify the measures to be used to assess progress.

This process is very different from traditional business discussions. Everyone knows how to conduct business within the traditional paradigm; changing to a new business process is threatening. What is the new work? What are we supposed to do? Will we be successful? What are the rewards if we are successful? What are the consequences if we are not? All the while you are learning and doing this new work, you have to do the old work as well because your company will not simply abandon current, ongoing activities. For a limited time, it is often necessary to run parallel systems while experimenting with the new business practices.

BARRIERS AND BENEFITS

"The concept is really pretty simple and straightforward, but the individual nuances and scenarios that arise between any two companies take some time to understand. It's not a part-time focus."

Art Karrer, Pharmavite Corporation, *Food Logistics and Retailtech,* Fall 2001

As you begin this new collaborative process, the first question is, "How do you develop trust with a partner with whom you have never had trust?" Someone needs to take the first step and begin sharing information, always remembering to keep the conversation focused on consumer needs. The research conducted by Kurt Salmon Associates for the ECR committee stated that it takes about nine to twelve months to begin establishing trust.[8] This is not an easy process.

As the company teams begin to work together, misunderstanding of criteria, objectives, or processes may create confusion. Prioritizing projects is an important task. The joint team needs to choose work that will make a significant difference. The team needs to spend time describing the activities that will be encompassed by the project, agreeing upon goals, and specifying measures to be used when assessing the results. This process will take some time, but if these decisions are not articulated early, the process will fall apart later.

Several problems may surface as joint teams begin to work together: (1) the culture of one organization may be less collaborative than the other, (2) the two companies may not have similar goals, (3) the focus may drift from the consumers' needs, or (4) one company does not have a sense of urgency about the project.[9] Any of these barriers makes it difficult for a company to coordinate front- and back-office activities within its own organization in a way that allows for good speed in creating a plan and implementing it in the marketplace. Collaboration will not move forward unless these issues are resolved.

"If you're able to level production and you don't have 'spikes' in the manufacturing plant, you should be able to cut down the plant capacity 10 percent to 15 percent. But that required having about 40% of volume up and running with CPFR, and that's going to take awhile."

Jack Haedicke,
Arena Consulting,
Food Logistics and Retailtech, Fall 2001

One example of a collaborative experiment that is struggling is Covisint, an e-marketplace for the automotive industry.[10] Covisint began with the goal of having all member companies share the cost of creating a central public e-marketplace for the automotive industry. GM, Ford, Oracle, and Commerce One promised to coordinate and manage a common set of software packages for the industry to use. However, its vision expanded to allow for hosting private exchanges for companies and providing portal services to purchasing sites that are fully operated by big manufacturers. Only 5 percent of companies in the automotive industry are registered and there are signs of technical disagreement. In addition, BMW, Honda, Robert Bosch, Toyota, Volkswagen, and others began constructing their own private exchanges. This collaborative initiative has not been very successful up to this point. Some critics suggest that the companies became distracted by money and began to lose focus on the final consumer. There are no common standards for data exchange in this industry and no agreement about what body or organization should set standards. At this point, progress on collaborative projects in this situation is not promising.

The annual survey of 145 U.S. companies on supply chain collaboration by Meta Group found that while some barriers are related to technology and technical standards, many are related to lack of trust, cultural resistance, lack of awareness, lack of commitment by top management, or lack of vendor support (see Table 9.2).[11]

Costs

What are the costs of this collaborative paradigm? First, the training cost is high, but critical for success. All the employees need to know how to use any new systems or technology. Second, there is the cost for employees' time to attend training. Third, there is a cost for equipment and technology (point-of-sale equipment, satellites, computers, etc.). Fourth, there is a cost for education so that all employees know what changes are occurring and why, especially since this activity cuts across many functions.

TABLE 9.2. Top Ten Biggest Barriers to High-Tech Supply Chain Management Collaboration*

Score	Topic
6.80	Technology/integration cost/complexity
6.63	Lack of trading partner technology sophistication
6.55	Lack of clear benefits/ROI
6.26	Cultural resistance to new trading partner paradigms
5.97	Until recently, few native Web-centric applications designed for this collaboration
5.85	Lack of technical standards
5.68	Fear of divulging proprietary information to business partners
5.51	Lack of awareness of solutions
5.46	Lack of commitment by top management
5.35	Lack of vendor support for collaborative processes

Source: Reprinted with permission from "Up the Down Supply Chain," *Marketing News,* published by the American Marketing Association, Meta Group, Inc., September 10, 2001, p. 3.

*Scale of 1 to 10 with 10 being the biggest barrier

Benefits of Collaboration

While the implementation process is not easy, the benefits result in improved business practices and increased business.[12] First, companies find that they understand their business partners better—why they do things a certain way, why they process information in a certain way, or why they cannot provide data in a certain format. Second, the joint discussion produces better alignment on common goals—people representing all the relevant business functions hear the background discussion, can ask questions of clarification, and understand the rationale behind the new work required of them. Third, specifying metrics creates a way to measure progress—the members of the team can assess progress and determine whether the project was successful. Fourth, and most important, the discussion between partners becomes strategic—instead of making decisions based on deals or new promotions, the members make decisions based upon whether specific activities will result in a more efficient way of meeting consumers' needs and adding **value.**[13]

"Speed—in seeing what's happening, in anticipating it, in responding to it—is the essence."

Rick Carmen, Managing Director, Dechert-Hamp & Co., www.ideabeat.com, August 8, 2001

Some of the initial pilot studies demonstrated specific benefits. For instance, in a survey of 361 companies in 1995, results indicated that inventory decreased, throughput of cases increased, sales increased, and gross dollars increased.[14] Once these benefits were publicized, more companies began to pursue collaborative activities.

True Value services over 7,000 independent retailers, uses 2,500 vendors, and has fourteen distribution centers in the hardware and home center industry. True Value's supply network situation was such that vendor service level was 75 percent, service level to the customer was 85 percent, vendor lead time was twenty-eight days, and it took five days for products to move from dock to in-stock. With dissatisfied customers and cash flow pressure, True Value began working with eight vendors to create joint business plans. The overall objectives were to create good sales forecasts, identify exceptions, and collaborate on exception items. When implementing the joint plan, vendors became inventory analysts making decisions on what product comes into the retail outlets and when. As a result, True Value took $100 million out of inventory across the distribution network. Gross sales increased 10 to 20 percent, outbound and inbound logistics transportation costs decreased 10 to 30 percent, promotional service levels increased, and the forecast accuracy and service levels to the stores improved.[15] With this success, True Value planned to expand the process to additional vendors.

"Without question, CPFR is the real thing."

Joseph C. Andraski, Former Vice President, Customer Marketing Operations, Nabisco Supplement to *Food Logistics and Retailtech,* Fall 2001

Many companies are installing Collaborative Planning, Forecasting, and Replenishment (CPFR) software, which enables trading partners to develop a market-specific plan for doing business jointly and profitably. Retailers provide proprietary information, e.g., sales forecasts and point-of-sale data, to their suppliers who produce sales forecasts with the objective of matching consumer demands with supply.[16] In 1999 Kmart and Kimberly-Clark began using this approach and were able to identify a rolling forecast for fifty-two weeks and a promotional sales forecast for seventeen weeks. With these forecasts, the partners monitored sales to spot any deviation from the forecast and made changes in orders based upon what consumers had actually purchased. The partners were able to reduce excess inventories and increase in-stock availability by comparing actual sales with forecasted sales.

"All you need to do is correct one misaligned promotional order, and CPFR pays for itself."

Dan Van Hammond, Vice President, Supply Chain Management, Kmart, *Consumer Goods Technology,* Feb. 2001

AMR Research, Inc., found that both manufacturers and retailers benefit when using CPFR processes.[17] The manufacturers increased replenishment cycles by 12 to 30 percent, increased sales from 2 to 10 percent, and increased customer service by 5 to 10 percent. Retailers increased shelf stock rates by 2 to 8 percent, increased sales from 5 to 20 percent, and lowered logistics costs by 3 to 4 percent. This type of improvement not only takes out cost but also lowers the necessity for emergency production runs and emergency transportation to retailers.[18]

Being able to more accurately forecast and monitor inventory based on consumer purchases increases efficiency and reduces inventory cost in the supply chain. However, the costs and processes related to transportation are also a problem. Transportation costs are about 6 percent of revenue on average and many trucks are either not full when delivering or are empty when returning.[19] For instance, Land O'Lakes reports that 60 to 70 percent of all routes are shipped at less than truckload and that 50 percent of all trucks return empty. Collaborative transportation could optimize trucking and other transportation assets. While Coke and Pepsi might never collaborate on a route, both companies might be willing to collaborate with another company, such as Agilent, a maker of medical equipment. General Mills, Kraft, Nabisco, Procter & Gamble, and Quaker Oats are experimenting with a collaborative transportation system that could cut 4 to 10 percent off transportation costs. Using this process, different companies can consolidate small shipments into near-full truckloads or back haul goods rather than returning empty.

"Net Markets are redifining the way commerce is transacted. Shared intelligence is the only competitive weapon that counts. And collaboration is the only way to get it."

Food Logistics and Retailtech, Fall 2001

SUMMARY

Many collaborative experiments are under way; many companies are expanding collaborative activities after successful trials. One critical factor for success is a set of technical standards so data can be exchanged among partners. Retailers and manufacturers must make an investment in technology, people, and training. However, an essential factor for success is ensuring that these investments are made with the company's mission in mind. Progress is possible only if you know where you are going.

Where you are going must be consistent with consumers' interests or you will go out of business. Consumers control not only what they purchase, when they purchase, and the form of delivery but will also pay only what they consider to be a fair price. Your company needs to be organized so that consumers can interact with your company using their medium of choice in a seamless manner. By basing replenishment decisions on consumer purchases, companies are developing more efficient, cost-effective, seamless supply chains. Transferring data between companies, identifying best prices, or evaluating alternative products or services is not always straightforward or easy. Intermediaries play an important role

"Collaboration is here to stay. . . . If done right, it rips cost out of the supply chain. It ensures that the right products arrive on time. And if a customer walks into your store and finds what they want, when they want it, they're happy to shop your store instead of someone else's, which means higher sales all the way around."

Jeff Smith, Managing Partner for e-Business, Consumer Goods Services, Andersen Consulting, *Food Logistics,* Nov./Dec. 2000 in making connections between companies or between companies and consumers.

"Every morning in Africa a gazelle wakes up . . . it knows it must run faster than the fastest lion or it will be killed. Every morning a lion wakes up . . . it knows it must outrun the slowest gazelle or it will starve to death. It doesn't matter whether you are a lion or gazelle . . . when the sun comes up, you'd better be running."

Aligning business processes internally and developing collaborative business processes does result in increased efficiencies. If these practices are also based upon consumers' needs, choices, and preferences, the result is success. Since consumers change, your company must not only be prepared to monitor consumer shifts in attitudes and preferences but also continue to change business processes to satisfy consumer needs in a cost-effective way.

The new business paradigm is not the adoption of best business practices in isolation, but a journey, as your company develops better business practices collaboratively—always keeping your eye on the consumer.

* * *

"[T]he customer is the only one who can fire all of us. . . ."

Sam Walton

Section IV: Real World Applications

"Widespread use of the Internet and allied technologies will fundamentally change the way we handle our business at home and at the office. It will collapse the many expensive layers of administrative, marketing, and distribution bureaucracy, much as the assembly-line revolution greatly reduced production costs. Electronic communication and commerce will also allow companies to tailor products and services to individual needs for what standardized goods cost today. Customized goods and services, once luxuries, will increasingly be affordable for the average consumer. The result is that consumers will get better products at better prices because businesses will be able to customize and cut costs."

Harry S. Dent Jr. (1998)
The Roaring 2000s

The companies on the superhighway have adopted consumer-centric business processes and are implementing the tools discussed in this book. These companies have experienced success, are convinced this is the future, and are continuing on the journey. The companies on the on-ramp are beginning to implement some of the processes and tools. They experience some frustration and success. They move forward in fits and starts. Sometimes they lose direction and need encouragement. The last third of companies have not adopted a consumer-centric approach and are busy responding to crises and cutting costs.

None of the companies uses all the tools; none of the companies focuses on all areas. Depending upon its mission and consumers' needs, each company chooses the tools and processes that will be most effective for ensuring its success. The first chapter in this section of the book presents a number of vignettes describing how companies adopted a particular tool or process that generated success for them. The other chapter in this section presents questions that are most often asked of the authors regarding a consumer-centric approach to doing business or the use of specific processes or tools.

Chapter 10

Success Stories

With the widespread use of credit cards and access to the Internet, consumers are now in the position of power. They can purchase products or services from retailers, distributors, intermediaries, or manufacturers when they want, to be delivered when and how they want, at a price they are willing to pay. This statement fundamentally alters the business environment. Consumers do not have to patronize local retail outlets; consumers do not have to go to a retail location to order products and services; consumers expect to use the communication vehicle (fax, phone, Internet, or in person) that is most convenient for them at a particular point in time; consumers expect that all channels of communication used by a specific company will be coordinated with one another; retailers and manufacturers must figure out how to get their message, products, and services to the consumers rather than waiting for consumers to come to them; collaboration **AND** competition are required for success. These changes require efficient flows of information, product, and money, thereby necessitating a change in business processes.

The grocery and consumer packaged goods industries embarked on a major, industry-wide initiative in 1992 and that included analysis of the current environment, identification of potential cost savings, creation and reporting of pilot studies testing new business processes, and the publication of forty-plus best practices books. This intensive activity involving the whole industry and all members of the supply chain from producer through consumer identified, tested, and promulgated new business processes. Other industries, such as hardware, food service, and health care, created their own initiatives to investigate new business processes.

While the industries may differ, an essential common thread among the applications tested and the success stories reported here is the focus on satisfying consumer needs and wants. Companies need to balance the need to individualize products or services offered to consumers with the need to cut costs and/or improve efficiency. In addition, companies in the demand and supply chain need to collaborate with one another when creating business processes that balance the competing demands.

Specific demands, challenges, and barriers may differ across industries, products, and environments. However, the principle of creating consumer-centered business processes is a common thread. The examples presented in this chapter demonstrate the applicability of the consumer-centric concept across industries, companies, and business situations. Adaptation to the business environment and flexibility in meeting consumer needs and wants are critical factors for success. However, the belief in a need for adaptation based upon specific consumer requirements is the foundation of the changing business processes.

RITE AID

Almost eight months after becoming chairman and chief executive officer of Rite Aid Corp., Bob Miller said that if he had known the extent of the drug chain's problems before joining the company, he would not have joined.[1] Top management created a strategy calling for initiatives under six broad headings: taking care of customers, treating employees right, honing product offerings to boost front-end sales, improving the image of Rite Aid's pharmacy operations, running first-rate stores, and building credibility with vendors. Miller convinced the retailer's three groups of creditors to be patient. The proposed program yielded steadily rising sales and operating earnings.

SOUTHWEST AIRLINES

Last year Southwest Airlines' share of traffic among the nine major U.S. airlines was 6.6 percent while it generated 90 percent of the country's low-fare competition.[2] Southwest's decision to keep all workers and continue its flying schedule could have significant consequences for consumers, affecting fares and services from short hops to transcontinental routes. It will probably expand into more long-haul markets, even bringing lower business fares to transcontinental services. It could emerge from the industry's troubles bigger and stronger. Southwest's profit formula relies on keeping costs low—it skimps on meals—and squeezing the maximum profit out of its aircraft use. It does this mainly by unloading and loading planes in just twenty minutes.

STARBUCKS

Starbucks is an excellent example of really understanding consumers and competes by meeting the individual's *moment of value*.[3] First, Starbucks branded a concept—Starbucks equals gourmet coffee. Starbucks created a desire for a niche item by putting tiny stores everywhere, in every nook and cranny where its consumers are, developing a direct mail channel including a coffee-of-the-month club and a virtual store, putting kiosks in airports, and becoming the exclusive coffee provider on United Airlines flights. With this ingenuity, Starbucks gets better margins and the ability to reach its target consumers in yet another time and place—at yet another *moment of value*. To keep innovating in response to consumer preferences, Starbucks tries a new idea in one store; if it's popular, it's rolled out to other stores.

GOLDEN CAT

Golden Cat piloted continuous replenishment in 1993 with a number of its distributor and retail customers including H. E. Butt Grocery Co., Hannaford Bros. Co., and Wegman's Food Markets, Inc.[4] One of the company's most successful partnerships has been with Schnuck Markets, Inc. The result of a category review that examined the total market profile, trends, and the role of cat box filler in its pet aisle strategy was that a lot of money had been invested in this category and it wasn't doing much with it. Today Schnuck's is practicing continuous replenishment with forty-five vendors, accounting for 50 percent of its core grocery volume. Turn rates of products using continuous replenishment have increased anywhere from 20 to 350 percent.

SNAP-ON

Snap-on hand tools comprise about 40 percent of the company's product line; they also sell diagnostic systems, automotive lifts, alignment systems, diagnostic software, detailed vehicle service information, and training material and services to automotive technicians worldwide.[5] In the mid-1990s, Bob Cornog, Snap-on's CEO, had a vision to expand Snap-on's presence from individual repair technicians and their repair shops to industrial customers as well as the emerging market of skilled do-it-yourselfers. He wanted to increase the company's global reach, and he wanted to evolve its product line from tools alone to diagnostic systems and software as well as everything else technicians needed to do their jobs. By early 1998 Bob Cornog had realized that the Internet and e-commerce could move Snap-on further toward his "store without walls" vision.

To create a single e-commerce infrastructure to reach out to all of Snap-on's different customer sets and channel partners, Snap-on worked to link consumers and dealers directly into the company's new enterprise computer systems, giving them real-time access to inventory and pricing, letting them place orders online, and reviewing the status of their orders. Beginning with product information, computer hardware and software were used to create a "store without walls"; consumers (dealers and end consumers) could purchase products directly on the Internet, interact with Snap-on employees, or get support on special dealer Web sites. In the first three months of operation, 90,000 people registered on Snap-on's consumer Web site. Snap-on's U.S. dealers are in contact with almost 80 percent of the market.

Snap-on has single-mindedly pursued its vision of offering a consistent branded experience to professional technicians around the world. Keeping dealers happy is vital to the continued success of Snap-on's total customer experience. Snap-on now offers its consumers the ultimate in convenience: shop online and have the product delivered to you by mail or by your friendly Snap-on dealer when he comes to your shop this week. Consumers can shop online and return products that don't meet their needs. Consumers can shop in the van, touch and feel the products, and get advice or e-mail their dealer for advice in the middle of the night.

Snap-on's total consumer experience is strong because it's a multitouchpoint, multichannel experience with a strong human touch. They have done an excellent job of rolling out a single, integrated infrastructure for all channels and touchpoints. As Snap-on tackled channels—first its industrial customers, then the new consumer channel, then its dealers and their customers, e-market makers, and other channel partners—the company kept life simple by using a single, unified product database. No matter who a customer is or what channel he comes through, the individual will have the identical customer experience with Snap-on's products and offerings while seeing the pricing that is appropriate for that consumer.

DOROTHY LANE

The Dorothy Lane store in Dayton, Ohio, makes the best of limited space with its 15,000 square-foot store in a middle-class neighborhood.[6] The store has many solutions: prepared meals, in-store chefs, a great bakery (famous for "Killer

Brownies"), its own Starbucks-like coffee bar, great meat and fish, a floral department, and on and on. In the traditional center-store categories, Dorothy Lane favors variety over redundancy. For example, there are only three plain yellow mustard SKUs—the two most popular brands, one in two sizes—along with one each of several specialty mustards.

GIANT EAGLE AND HUBERT CO.

Private trading networks represent a new tool to link the interests of buyers, suppliers, and distribution partners. Giant Eagle and Hubert Co. collaborated on development of a private trading network.[7] Under the new system, Giant Eagle purchasing agents are able, via a secure Web connection, to access the Hubert Co. electronic catalog and order small wares online. The new exchange has made the entire ordering and purchasing process a lot more efficient and faster; all the paperwork has been taken out of the system, resulting in savings of up to 20 percent. While the initial promise is low cost, the ultimate value comes through effective cooperation that benefits all parties. Steven Tassaro, a Giant Eagle vice president, said that while it took about one year to put the new system together, the user is now in control. The buying specialist goes online, enters a password, places an order, and the whole transaction is secure—complete with a bill-to-ship for more than 2,000 small ware items.

Hubert Co. has established similar private exchanges with Marriot Hotels and Restaurants and cites advantages of reduced paperwork, getting orders to stores faster, better reports and real-time tracking status, streamlining the processing of invoices, and consistency among stores.

NATIONAL SEMICONDUCTOR

National Semiconductor is becoming known for its innovative e-business initiatives, all of which are designed to save customers' time.[8] They have built deep customer relationships with three distinct sets of target customers: those who influence the purchase of its products (e.g., design engineers); those who actually do the purchasing (e.g., purchasing agents); and the distributors through whom purchasers procure not just National parts but the complete bills of materials they need for each product they're going to manufacture.

Today, half of the world's design engineers visit National's Web site at least once a month. Fifty-eight percent of the traffic on the site is international. Customers download 400,000 data sheets per month, place 21,000 orders per month, use seven different search tools, interact in ten different languages, and receive 48,000 Web referrals per month from customers who not only are qualified but have already selected the products they want to buy.

In 1999, National launched its first truly ambitious customer scenario: a series of tools that enabled engineers to design power supplies for the products they were building. When consumers were asked what they wanted next, there were two answers: have a way to do thermal simulations of the complete design and be able to design more of the phone's circuitry online. The company has been zealous about measuring what matters to customers. Phil Gibson began by watching the click-stream traffic on the site and analyzing the patterns. As soon as he could tell what customers were trying to do, he would concentrate on eliminating all unnecessary clicks. Every morning, he gets a list of the top 200 search terms used by customers the day before and what results were yielded. He looks through the list carefully to see what changes need to be made to the site that day to make it easier for customers to find what they're seeking. There is an additional bonus from this practice: as soon as customers start searching his site for a competitor's part he catches it on the first day. The company also measures and monitors the number of design simulations customers do. By being involved at the front end of the design process, National is better able to predict which devices it will need to manufacture in quantity.

National's business is currently growing 30 percent a year. The value added is increasing from $2 per phone to $20 per phone as the circuitry for the devices becomes more integrated. If consumers commit to National's circuitry early in their design cycle, it is highly unlikely that they'll take the time to switch suppliers in mid-design. Based on more than eighteen months of experience, National knows that it has saved its customers an average of forty-three hours per design for an average savings of $2,580. In the first year these tools were offered, customers did 20,800 designs for a total customer savings of more than $53 million. More important than the dollars saved were the time savings and the design efficiencies for customers. Customers are now able to do hundreds of iterations of each design in the time it used to take for them to finalize a single design.

What Phil Gibson and his team have done is to put themselves in their customers' shoes and figure out how they can save them time in the most valuable parts of their jobs. Customers become partners and make suggestions for the next set of innovations they would like to see. National's team implements the suggestions and offers every step the customer needs to do, including the cost/benefit analysis, running the design simulation, preparing a bill of materials, ordering the parts, and testing the design. In addition, if the customer needs access to non-National parts, not only does National provide that information, it links the customer directly to the distributors that have those parts in stock.

EATZI'S

eatZi's is an 8,000 square-foot "store" in Dallas developed by Brinker International.[9] eatZi's bridges the gap between supermarkets and restaurants by offering products from both, including masterfully merchandised fresh prepared entrées, salads, and baked goods along with limited grocery items such as beverages and snacks. Twelve chefs staff the flagship store at all times, and the dinner hour routinely causes traffic jams in the parking lot. The company has opened stores in Houston, Atlanta, New York, Long Island, and Maryland.

SIEMENS

Siemens used to make the toughest telephones in the world, constructed by engineers so bent on quality that they designed and produced their own screws.[10] Early mobile phones took workers at the German giant thirteen hours to produce. Not many consumers wanted to pay for that kind of phone and, by 1998, Siemens had slipped to ninth place worldwide among mobile phone makers and was losing money. The German manufacturing conglomerate, which makes everything from gas-turbine generators to streetcars to lightbulbs, has always had great engineers who developed products and hoped somebody would buy them. Siemens has since learned that success also requires marketing, up-to-date design, and ruthless attention to costs. CEO Henrich von Pierer is trying to hard-wire the ideas of speed, innovation, and customer-pleasing products into the company's collective consciousness. Joint committees of engineers and marketers oversee new-product development, cooperating on ways to grab customers' attention, outsourcing manufacturing jobs not essential to the company, and jumping on new ideas, even if the competition comes up with them first. By 2000, Siemens' C35i mobile phones were sliding off an assembly line one every seven seconds. Each phone requires five minutes to produce. This renovation process was painful but the payoff is obvious. Profits are soaring and share price has doubled from 1999. A massive e-commerce push will let Siemens conduct 50 percent of consumer-oriented sales online within a few years, saving billions. Teaching Siemens the rules of the New Economy hasn't always been easy, says Unisphere COO Tom Burkardt who complains that Siemens is still burdened with too many middle managers who resist change.

TESCO

Tesco is a U.K. based global supermarket chain.[11] The large supermarket chains are battling for their share of families' stomachs and many of them compete on price. Tesco is competing on customer loyalty and customer experience. Its prices are competitive in each local market so customers get a fair deal. Equally important, Tesco knows who its customers are and deepens its relationships with them over time. Tesco measures and monitors what matters to customers, including which items are close to out-of-stock, how quickly its delivery vans make it through traffic, and how it performs relative to various Internet service points across the country.

In late 1997 Tesco Direct was still primarily a call-center-based operation. Gary Sargeant turned his attention to streamlining operations and tweaking the business so he could offer online shopping profitably. The model being used was the in-store fulfillment model, so each customer would purchase online from the store in which he or she would normally shop in person, receiving the same price for each item online as the price in the store nearest his or her home. This approach keeps regional pricing variations and allows prices to be competitive with those charged by local stores. By linking the online shopping applications directly to each store's inventory systems, it was unlikely that customers would order a product that was not available. In addition, consumers were familiar with what products were available in their local stores. Servers in each store could also save a history of each consumer's favorite products to ensure that they were always in stock.

The "basket mix" of Tesco's online shoppers is two to three percentage points more profitable than the average customer's in-store market basket. The shopping site does a good job of cross-selling and up-selling. When a consumer checks off an item (like bread), other related items (such as marmalade or butter) pop up on the screen. The Tesco Direct team takes the customer experience very seriously. They monitor on-time deliveries, accuracy of orders, and customer satisfaction. They simulate customers' online shopping experiences to proactively monitor the state of the end-to-end customer experience. This constant monitoring of the conditions that customers are facing helps Tesco proactively sort out problems as they occur.

OTIS ELEVATOR

Otis is one of the most famous brands in the world, with customers in more than 200 countries, and has operated a standard corporate Web site for years—mostly in

English and not interactive.[12] By 2000 management agreed that it was time to upgrade Otis's Web presence in order to increase sales and lower marketing costs. There were the logistical challenges of creating dozens of national Web sites and the internal politics of getting marketers and sales reps around the world to buy into the project. First, the team had to decide whether to create separate Web sites for each country or one giant Otis site for the whole world. They decided to create a global site to create a global image. Besides, installing, maintaining, and managing 200 Web sites around the world would be very cost-inefficient. The development team created a series of templates for creating local Web sites within Otis.com:

- Common navigation bars (in twenty-six languages initially)
- Standardized page layouts
- Rules limiting individual page content sizes to 30k each for speedy load times
- Interactive features, including user registration and a "Plan Your Project" tool
- A series of e-mail-based request-for-information forms that fed into a centralized e-mail management system, which in turn fed out to local customer service and sales reps
- Each national headquarters was asked to select a staff person to be in charge of Web content management and a marketer to be in charge of Web-related marketing

Many sales reps initially felt threatened by the idea of changing from traditional sales to an e-business culture. As sales figures came in, it was clear that the clients and prospects that used the interactive project planning tools at the site ended up being bigger and better accounts. So, Otis sales reps were asked to help their clients set up their first project plan at the site during personal sales calls. Otis started measuring sales reps' success by reporting on the number of saved projects per client, per rep, and per local region. Otis also started measuring the amount of time it took for each site-generated e-mail inquiry to be answered by a real human. To encourage faster responses, local sites are measured against each other.

Since the first revised global site launch in March 2000, Otis.com's traffic has grown 150 percent to 120,000 unique monthly visitors. With the help of a now-eager sales team, an astonishing 67 percent of unique visitors are registered members. The interactive features of the sites have been an enormous success. Registered members have used the interactive project planning process to create and budget for more than 20,000 Otis purchases. People who plan a project online are far more likely to end up purchasing from Otis. The number of e-mailed requests for information generated through Otis.com has grown nearly tenfold. Approximately 40 to 50 percent of e-mails received are solid sales leads. Once the sales reps began to see how valuable these leads were, their average response time dropped dramatically. The amount of money spent on print materials was cut substantially. Expensive direct mail campaigns are now considered just "supplemental" to site marketing. Plus, the introduction of new promotions has accelerated, because marketers can add special offers to the site—such as something free with order during the next thirty days—quickly and easily without waiting for art, mail, or printing. Marketers in twenty-one countries have begun "narrowcasting" e-mailed promotions and newsletters to registered site visitors in their region. Data-mining reports show visitors interacting with the site in order to learn how to make it more effective.

Chapter 11

Frequently Asked Questions

Changing to a new business paradigm is not a decision made lightly or in haste. Choosing to focus business decisions and strategies on providing value to consumers involves new business processes, new business activities, integration of new technology, and new reward systems. Questions abound when first learning about this new business paradigm, when beginning to implement new business processes, and when implementing specific activities. In this chapter, we present some of the most frequently asked questions and responses to them.

What's new? We have always been focused on the customer. . . . Our motto is "the customer is always right."

Both the supplier and the distributor recognize that neither has the "power" and know that all the power has shifted to the consumer who decides what to buy, when to buy, where to buy, and how much to pay. Realizing that the customer can and will purchase products and services from other vendors outside the immediate geographic location widens the span of competition, can decrease loyalty to local retail outlets, and intensifies the **importance of value.** Developing business processes that enable company representatives to develop a relationship with consumers to provide immediate responsiveness and individualization in any format goes far beyond customer satisfaction. This paradigm shift encompasses new business processes, focusing all business activities and decisions on providing value to consumers.

Isn't this whole process—call it ECR, JIT, QR, or whatever—just a fad or consultants' dream for making money?

In an ideal world, we would not put a name or moniker on any of this. We believe the entire emphasis needs to be placed on **changing the business process,** changing the way product flows, the way information flows, and the way cash flows.

When all is said and done, don't the customers just want the lowest price?

Survey after survey indicates that consumers really want **VALUE** for their money. That **value equation** can include service, freshness, in-stock conditions, convenience, entertainment, and **FAIR** prices, not just the lowest price.

If 51 percent of the profit for wholesalers comes from the "inside margin" of deals, promotions, forward buying, diverting, slotting allowances, etc., where will profit come from if we eliminate this old business model?

Wholesalers are rethinking the way they go to market and are in the process of "unbundling" charges for their retailers so the efficient operators get the benefits and the inefficient pay a penalty. They also must position themselves as supply chain leaders and provide services for self-distributing chains as well as independents.

Where do you add VALUE?

This is the key question for all participants in the demand chain. If you cannot clearly articulate your **value proposition,** you will be very vulnerable and your survival could well be threatened.

These new business processes seem to work well for the big companies who can afford the new technology and manpower to implement. How about the "little guy"? . . . Is he doomed and left in a noncompetitive position?

This is an interesting question. In the grocery industry, it was actually a very small operator (Golden Cat) who led the industry in changing the business process. The big guys need the little guys and stand ready to assist them in playing in this new arena by providing technology and technical assistance they can't afford.

What are the impediments and barriers? Which have been the most difficult to overcome?

There are several barriers, all of which can be overcome.

1. The most difficult is **TRUST** and trying to build new trust relationships in an environment that was built on adversarial, buy/sell relationships.
2. Another significant barrier is the reluctance or unwillingness to share data. Information has been considered power and companies consider their data to be proprietary and generally refuse to share their data.

3. Lack of senior management **visible** support will doom this to failure.
4. This must be a long-term commitment and resources must be allocated for both human and financial needs.
5. Traditional organizational structures are barriers inasmuch as the new business model requires a cross-functional team effort whereas the old model supports silo management where individuals and departments are the most important.
6. Old measurements and rewards must be abandoned in favor of new measurements and rewards that support the new business model. Failure to change will definitely result in people reverting back to the old model.

If everyone adopts this new business model, won't all companies be equal and lose any competitive advantage or differentiation?

That would be Utopia and it just does not happen that way. Today, after ten years in ECR, only 35 percent of companies in the food industry have truly adopted this new business model and have a significant competitive advantage. Another 35 percent are "working on it," and the last 30 percent will probably never get there and not survive.

If trust is so important in this new business strategy, how do you build trust in an environment that is based on adversarial buy/sell relationships and mistrust?

The real secret is to start with small successes, using teams from both the supplier and distributor to develop new efficiencies and best practices that result in adding **value** to the **mutual** consumer.

You say it is necessary to form the proper infrastructure (for companies, for countries, and for industries). . . . Can you describe those infrastructures specifically?

If you refer back to our technology chapter (Chapter 7), you will find reference to infrastructure changes required to support this new business process. These include hardware/software requirements as well as standardization in product coding, electronic data interchange transactions, case marketing symbology, pallet sizing, etc.

Do wholesalers have a future in the electronically linked, transparent model?

There are wholesalers succeeding and surviving in this new environment by rethinking their basic mission and business plan. They must have a value-added business proposition and they can play a very significant role in an industry where distribution and logistics are being consolidated and outsourced.

How do the dollars saved ultimately get allocated between the manufacturer and the distributors?

The dollars achieved through improved efficiencies don't get "allocated." The real intent is to pass on those savings in improved **value** to the consumer.

Is all of this change about technology or is it about people?

Recognizing that technology is having a significant impact on everything we do, one must also realize that the changes described in this book are only 20 percent about technology and 80 percent about people. The reason we say this is because we know the tremendous amount of time and effort that must be dedicated to the education, training, and retraining of people in order to facilitate all of these changes. The other "people" issue is the constant need for communication—keeping the entire organization informed of the new business paradigms and processes.

If the dollars saved are passed on to the consumer in the way of added value, how does the bottom line get enhanced?

If you are truly enhancing consumer **VALUE,** you will be building revenue through competitive advantage and, with the lower costs of improved efficiencies, you will be adding incremental net profits.

What are the current projections for online or Internet business?

That depends on who you are talking to on any given day. Realistically, the projections of 10 to 15 percent seem to be reasonable. The Internet is not going to dominate the business . . . there is going to be room for many other types of retail, including the traditional brick and mortar facilities.

Can you work* legally *in this new collaborative environment? What are the risks?

Sure, you have to stay legal! With the ECR initiative, the lawyers were present in every meeting and guided all discussions and writings to ensure legal compliance. The real risk is doing nothing for fear of legal entanglements.

Everyone seems to be adopting some sort of loyalty program or frequent buyer plan. . . . Is that the answer to success?

Obviously, a lot of businesses think it is, as evidenced by the numerous programs in existence today. However, extremely successful operations, such as Wal-Mart, believe it is unnecessary. Their contention is that success lies in treating **all of their** consumers fairly and not differentiating between consumers.

Wal-Mart just keeps getting bigger and more powerful. . . . Is there a future for anyone else?

Despite the fact that Wal-Mart has grown to more than $200 billion in revenues, there is hope and room for others. If you analyze markets where Wal-Mart has entered, there are many survivors and these are the operators who continue to find their niche and provide **value** for their consumers.

* * *

> "The relentless adherence to out-of-date business models endangers any and all companies that continue to try to insulate themselves from the future. . . . It will take nothing less than questioning every assumption on how business runs to fix what is broken."
>
> Ryan Mathews
> Grocery Headquarters
> April 2003

Notes

Chapter 1

1. Myers, Rich and Jennifer Fan (2001), "429 Million People Worldwide Have Internet Access, According to Nielsen/NetRatings," Nielsen/NetRatings, Stamford, CT (June 11).

2. Niles, Dan (2002), "PDAs Have Come a Long Way, Baby," <http://news.cnet.com/news/0-1273-210-3287333-1.html> (September 26); Charny, Ben (2001), "2002: A Merry New Year for Cell Phones?", <http://news.cnet.com/news/0-1004-200-7994720.html> (November 27).

3. Veiders, Christina (2001), "FDI Examines Impact of Consumer Trends on Distribution," *Supermarket News* (September 17), p. 6.

4. Ghitelman, David (2001), "Rush to Retail," *Supermarket News* (September 17), pp. 9, 12.

5. Vosburgh, Robert (2000), "Study: Food Service to Eclipse Retail in New Food Sales," *Supermarket News* (September 25), p. 39.

6. Singleton, Christopher J. (1992), "Auto Industry Jobs in the 1980's: A Decade of Transition," *Monthly Labor Review* (February), pp. 18-27.

7. "A Retailing Legend Is Born," Kmart History at <www.Kmart.com>, August 22, 2001; Donlon, J.P. (1995), "A Glass Act," *Chief Executive* (105) (July), pp. 40-49; Halverson, Richard (1996), "Global Growth Marked by Guarded Steps," *Discount Store News* (February 19), pp. 26, 46-48; Kmart's *Annual Report* (1994); Kmart's *Annual Report* (2000) (ending December 31, 2000) at <www.Kmart.com>; "Kmart Corp. Closing 3 Singapore Units" (1996), *Daily News Record,* 26(130) (July 9), p. 10; "Kmart Exits Europe" (1966), *WWD,* 171(45) (March 6), p. 30; Mander, Kai and Alex Boston (1995), "Wal-Mart Worldwide: The Making of a Global Retailer," *The Ecologist,* 25(6) (November/December), pp. 238-241; Pellet, Jennifer (1996), "Kmart's Eastern European Adventure," *Discount Merchandiser,* 36(4) (April), pp. 26-34; Wal-Mart's *Annual Report* (1994); Wal-Mart's *Annual Report* (2001) (ending January 31, 2001) at <www.Wal-Mart.com>; Walker, Richard (1985), "Kmart 1985 Profits Decline 56 Per Cent to $221 Million," *Business News* (August 19), Reuters.

8. ValleyoftheDamned.com (2000), *Food Logistics* (November/December).

Chapter 2

1. Schultz, Don E., Stanley I. Tannenbaum, and Robert F. Lauterborn (1994), *The New Marketing Paradigm,* Chicago, IL: NTC Business Books; "Profiles of General Demographic Characteristics" (2001), *2000 Census of Population and Housing,* U.S. Department of Commerce (May).

2. "Census 2000 Supplementary Survey Profile for United States" (2001), U.S. Census Bureau, <www.census.gov>, June 28; U.S. Bureau of Labor Statistics, Bulletin 2307.

3. "Profiles of General Demographic Characteristics" (2001), *2000 Census of Population and Housing,* U.S. Department of Commerce (May); "Census 2000 Supplementary Survey Profile for United States" (2001), U.S. Census Bureau, <www.census.gov>, June 28.

4. Russell, Cheryl (1999), "The New Consumer Paradigm," *American Demographics* (April), pp. 50-58.

5. Russell, "The New Consumer Paradigm," pp. 50-58.

6. "X Market's the Spot" (1995), *Discount Store News* 34(7) (April 3), p. 24; Miller, Cyndee (1995), "Retailers Do What They Must to Ring Up Sales," *Marketing News* 29(11) (May 22), pp. 1, 10-11; Mammarella, James (1995), "Choice and Image Key to Marketing X-cellence," *Discount Store News* 34(7) (April 3), p. 24.

7. Russell, "The New Consumer Paradigm."

8. Russell, "The New Consumer Paradigm."

9. Miller, "Retailers Do What They Must."

10. Spethman, Betsy (1997), "The Four O'Clock Dilemma: What's for Dinner?" *PROMO Magazine* (May), pp. 19-23.

11. Brandl, Phillip (1999), "Capture New Customers," *Discount Merchandiser* 29(1) (January), p. 48; Miller, "Retailers Do What They Must to Ring Up Sales"; Schulz, David P. (1994), "Top 100 Retailers: The Definitive Ranking," *Stores* 76(7) (July), pp. 16-32; "Wal-Mart Looks Ahead" (1994), *Discount Merchandiser* 34(7) (July), p. 16.

12. Kurt Salmon Associates, Inc. (1993), *Efficient Consumer Response: Enhancing Consumer Value in the Grocery Industry,* Washington, DC: Food Marketing Institute.

13. "Trends in the United States: Consumer Attitudes and the Supermarket" (1995), Food Marketing Institute; "Trends in the United States: Consumer Attitudes and the Supermarket" (1997), Food Marketing Institute.

14. Tigert, Douglas J. and Stephen J. Arnold (1994), "The Battle Continues: Target Greatlands and Wal-Mart Jump into Chicago," *Chain Store Age Executive* 7(8) (August), Section 3.

15. Salmon, Walter J. (1996), "Retailing at the Millennium: How Changes in Consumer Buying Behavior Are Driving Concentration," *International Trends in Retailing,* Retail Distribution Group of Arthur Andersen and Andersen Consulting (June), pp. 41-51.

16. Reagor, Catherine (2001), "Valley's New-Home Buyers Swayed by Service, Quality," *The Arizona Republic* (September 20), pp. D1, D2.

17. <www.newsdirectory.com> (2001) (September 7).

Chapter 3

1. A number of books have been written that describe cultural differences and business practices, such as *Culture and Organizations: Software of the Mind* by Geert Hofstede (1996, New York: McGraw-Hill Companies); *Global Business: Planning for Sales and Negotiations* by Camille P. Schuster and Michael J. Copeland (1996, Fort Worth: Dryden Press); *Managing Cultural Differences* by Philip R. Harris and Robert T. Moran (1991, Houston: Gulf Publishing Company); and *Riding the Waves of Culture* by Fons Trompenaars and Charles Hampden-Turner (1998, New York: McGraw-Hill Companies).

2. Jen, Danielle (2001), Presentation on Category Management at Arizona State University, East Morrison School of Agribusiness, February 22.

3. Rose, Frank (1999), "Think Globally, Script Locally," *Fortune* (November 8), pp. 157-160.

4. Goodman, Allan (2000), "IIE Briefing: Winter 2000," Institute of International Education (February 24); Luhnow, David (2001), "Lower Tariffs, Retail Muscle Translate into Big Sales for Wal-Mart in Mexico," <wjs.com>, (August 31).

Chapter 4

1. Terbeek, Glen (1999), *Agentry Agenda: Selling Food in a Frictionless Marketplace,* Chesterfield, VA: The American Book Company.

2. Mulholland, Sara (2001), "Survey Plots More or Less Successful Product Launches," *Supermarket News* (March 12), pp. 35, 38.

3. Tomkins, Richard (2001), "Baby-Boomers Eat Nutraceuticals to Fight Disease," *Financial Times,* <Business.com> (December 14).

4. "Ohio State Becomes Home of Soy Bread" (2001), *The Cincinnati Enquirer,* <http://enquirer.com/editions/2001/12/14/fin_ohio_state_becomes.html> (December 14).

5. Harrison, C. Richard (2001), "Design to Order," *Machine Design* (November 22).

6. Peppers, Don and Martha Rogers (1998), "Lessons from the Front," *Marketing Tools* (January/February), pp. 39-42.

7. "Del Monte Buys Sunfresh" (2000), *Retail NewsBeat,* <www.ideabeat.com> (August 29); Forster, Julie (2001), "Food," *BusinessWeek* (January 8), p. 129.

8. "USA: General Mills to Offer Create-Your-Own Cereal Website" (2001), <just.food.com> (December 10).

9. Landler, Mark (2001), "Hi, I'm in Bangalore (but I Dare Not Tell)," *The New York Times,* <222.nytimes.com> (March 21).

10. Berry, John (2001), "Marketing Automation Gives CRM A Lift," *In Depth,* <www.internetweek.com> (March 20).

11. Schwartz, Karen D. (2000), "Kraft Data Mining Transforms Marketing and Margins," *Consumer Goods Technology* (September), pp. 14-16.

12. "Marketing to Segments of ONE: Growth Opportunity" (2001), *Company Spotlights,* <www.ideabeat.com> (June 12).

13. Goldstein, Alan (2001), " 'Old Economy' Firms Adapt to E-Business," *The Arizona Republic* (January 14), pp. D1, D13.

14. Nelson, Emily (2001), "Too Many Choices," *The Wall Street Journal* (April 20), pp. B1, B4.

15. Nelson, "Too Many Choices."

16. Cortese, Amy (2001), "Masters of Innovation," *Business Week Online,* <www.businessweek.com> (March 23).

17. Warren, Susan (2001), " 'Smart' Fabrics Function Like Appliances: They Keep Track of Vital Signs, Hide Odor," *The Wall Street Journal,* <http://interactive.wsj.com> (August 10).

18. Craven, Scott (2001), "That's 1 Smart Shirt (Literally)," *The Arizona Republic* (September 21), pp. E1, E3.

19. McKay, Betsy (2000), "Pepsi Manages to Edge Past Coke by Capitalizing on Orange Juice," *The Wall Street Journal,* <http://interactive.wsj.com> (November 6).

20. Welch, Jack (1998), *The GE Way,* New York: Robert Slater and McGraw-Hill.

21. Cortese, "Masters of Innovation."

22. "Procter & Gamble Tests Tide of Household Services" (2001), *Retail NewsBeat,* <www.ideabeat.com> (February 14).

Chapter 5

1. Kurt Salmon Associates (1993), *Efficient Consumer Response: Enhancing Consumer Value in the Grocery Industry.* Washington, DC: Food Marketing Institute.

2. "Target Stores Adds Eddie Bauer" (2001), *Retail Merchandiser Online,* <www.retailmerchandiser.com> (January 22).

3. Faircloth, Anne (1998), "The Best Retailer You've Never Heard Of," *Fortune Online* (March 2).

4. Regan, Keith (2002), "Online Grocery Biz Still a War of Attrition," <www.EcommerceTimes.com> (March 15).

5. "Marketing to Segments of One: Customer Value" (2000), *Retail News,* <www.ideabeat.com/conceptshopping>.

6. "Keeping Customers Is Smart and Profitable" (2000), *Business Week,* Special Advertising Section (July 3).

7. Zwirin, Ed (2001), "Who's Mining the Data?" *Supermarket News* (March 19), pp. 19-20.

8. "Independents Take on Big Chains" (1998), *Progressive Grocer* (November), p. 13.

9. "Report Says Customer Satisfaction Declining" (2001), *Supermarket News* (February 26), p. 47.

10. <www.ac.com/new/newsarchive/1.00/newsarchive_011000.html>.

11. Alaimo, Dan (2001), "Hy-Vee Shopping Carts Going Wireless," *Supermarket News* (May 14), pp. 23-25; Longhran, Stephanie (2001), "Some Little Things Pay Off in Shopper Loyalty," *Supermarket News* (April 2), p. 18.

12. Kushner, David (1999), "Shock Village," *Village Voice* (November), pp. 3-9; Marriott, Michel (2000), "For Extra Cheese, Ctrl+Pizza," *The New York Times Online* (February 10).

13. Kiernan, Patrick (2000), "Online Auction: Coming Soon to Your Industry?" *Grocery Headquarters* (March), pp. 64-68; Hardgrove, Amy (2000), "Savoring the Experience," *Grocery Headquarters* (March), p. 65.

14. Graham, Alan (2001), "A Stroll Through the Apple Store," *O'Reilly Network* <www.oreillynet.com> (June 12); "Inside the Apple Store" (2001), <www.apple.com/retail/inside/html> (September 30).

15. Nannery, Matt (1999), "Braving New Worlds," *Chain Store Age* (September), pp. 69-78.

16. "Wal-Mart Cuts Prices on Another 1,000 Items in Germany" (2000), *Retail NewsBeat,* <www.retailnewsbeat.com> (August 29); "Wal-Mart Ordered to Stop Selling Below Cost in Germany" (2000), *Retail NewsBeat,* <www.retailnewsbeat.com> (September 11).

Chapter 6

1. Terbeek, Glen (1999), *The Agentry Agenda: Selling Food in a Frictionless Marketplace,* Chesterfield, VA: The American Book Company.

2. Zimmerman, Kim Ann (2001), "Beyond the Marketplace," *Food Logistics* (March 15), pp. 17-20.

3. Cortese, Amy (2001), "Masters of Innovation," *Business Week* <www.businessweek.com> (March 23).

4. Schwartz, Karen D. (2000), "The Importance of Brand Building on the Internet," *Consumer Goods Technology* (October), p. 24.

5. "The Internet—A Value-Added Opportunity" (2000), *Food Logistics* (November/December), p. 40.

6. Loudin, Amanda (2001), "Online Traffic Jam," *Food Logistics* (April 15), pp. 34-36.

7. Loudin, "Online Traffic Jam."

8. "Kroger to Tap Online Perishables Partnership by Spring" (2000), *Retail NewsBeat,* <www.ideabeat.com> (October 18).

9. "But . . . How Will the World Wide Retail Exchange, the Industry's Largest So Far, Fit into This?" (2001), *Retail NewsBeat,* <www.ideabeat.com> (January 9), p. 3.

Chapter 7

1. Stam, Nick (1999), "Moore's Law Will Continue to Drive Computing," *PC Magazine* (May 22), also at <http://www.zdnet.com/pcmag/features/future/moore01html>.

2. Joachim, David and Chuck Moozakis (2001), "Can Covisint Find Its Way?", <www.internetweek.com> (September 17); Lawton, George (2000), "Hygard Stitches Knowledge into Business Processes," *Consumer Goods Technology* (October), pp. 11-12.

3. Newburger, Eric C. (2001), "Home Computers and Internet Use in the United States: August 2000," *Current Population Reports* (September).

4. "Numbering Cyberspace" (2001), ITU Telecommunication Indicator Update (January/February/March).

5. "New Initiatives Enable the New Economy" (2000), *Consumer Goods Technology,* Supplement (October).

6. Greengard, Samuel (2001), "Making Contact," *IQ Magazine* (Summer), pp. 74-79.

7. Heubusch, Kevin (1998), "Welcome to the Machine," *Marketing Tools* (January/February), pp. 44-49.

8. Gomez Associates Study (2001), *Supermarket News* (April 2).

9. Perotta, Peter (2001), "Schnuck Anticipates Chainwide SBT Rollout," *Supermarket News* (January 8), pp. 18-23.

10. EMS ad (2001), in *The Wall Street Journal* (March 15).

11. Robinson, Alan (2001), "For 3PLs, the Jury Is Still Out on Exchanges," *Food Logistics* (January/February), pp. 44-46.

12. "Sync or Swim: Conducting Business Online" (2001), IdeaBeat's Company Spotlights, <www.ideabeat.com> (August 29); Schneider, Maria (2001), Presentation to MBA Class at Xavier University (March).

13. "Kraft, Shaw's Successfully Synchronize Product Data" (2001), *Food Logistics* (April 15).

14. Alaimo, Dan (2001), "Landmark E-Commerce Standards Will Be Released," *Supermarket News* (June 11), pp. 17-18; Drayer, Ralph (2001), Presentation to Executive MBA Class, Williams College of Business, Xavier University (April 20); Karolefsky, John (2001), "Collaborating Across the Supply Chain," *Food Logistics and Retailtech,* Supplement (Fall), pp. 24-34.

15. Karpinski, Richard (2002), "Travel Group Delivers Industry XML Standards," <www.internetweek.com> (February 26).

16. "Numbering Cyberspace" (2001), ITU Telecommunication Indicators Update (January/February/March).

17. Bartlar, Dennis (2001), "Global Village," <www.line56.com> (August 15); Williams, Frances (2001), "Chinese Tipped a Main Language of Web by 2007," <Ft.com> (December 6).

18. Fleischer, Jo (2001), "Companies Urged to Scrap Legacy Systems," *Supermarket News* (April 2), p. 39.

19. Schwartz, Karen D. (2000), "Merging ERP with E-Business at Mott's," *Consumer Goods Technology* (September), p. 7.

20. Morphy, Erika (2001), "CRM: Feeling the Pain," <www.crmdaily.com> (September 20); "CRM: Keeping Customers Loyal" (2000), *Business Week,* Special Advertising Section (July 3); "*Tried & True* Beats Out *New Econmomy* Tools by 2:1" (2001). Bain and Company's Eighth Annual "Management Tools" Survey, <www.bain.com> (June 13).

21. Vaas, Lisa (2002), "Cutting the Fat from CRM Implementation," eWeek, 19(2) (January 14); Boyd, Jade, Ted Kemp, and Margie Senniloff (2001), "IT Says No to CRM Integration," <www.internetweek.com> (November 12).

22. Lawton, George (2000), "Hygard Stitches Knowledge into Business Processes," *Consumer Goods Technology* (October), pp. 11-12.

23. Prencipe, Loretta W. (2001), "Taking Stock with P&G," <www.infoworl.com> (November 20).

24. "*Tried & True* Beats Out *New Economy* Tools by 2:1" (2001), Bain and Company's Eighth Annual "Management Tools" Survey, <bain.com> (June 13).

Chapter 8

1. These six factors are part of an Organization Performance Model presented in Hanna, Dave (1998), *Designing Organizations for High Performance,* Boston, MA: Addison-Wesley.

2. Purdum, Mike (Director of Retail Operations) (2001), Presentation to Williams College of Business MBA Class at Xavier University (April).

3. Maselli, Jennifer (2001). "People Problems," <Informationweek.com>, July 9.

4. Ibid.

5. Ibid.

6. Ibid.

7. Ibid.

8. "Johnson & Johnson's Integrated CRM Initiatives," *Consumer Goods Technology,* Supplement (April 2001), pp. 19-20.

9. Gorman, Cleve, Vice President of Strategic Planning at The Kroger Co. (1996, 1997) and Mike Purdum, (2001), Presentations to Williams College of Business MBA Students at Xavier University.

10. "Finding the True Value of Cost Benefits" (2001), *Food Logistics and RetailTech,* Supplement, p. 22; Purdum, Mike (Director of Retail Operations) (2001), Presentation to Williams College of Business MBA Class at Xavier University (April); Gorman, Cleve, Vice President of Strategic Planning at The Kroger Co. (1996, 1997), Presentations to Williams College of Business MBA Students at Xavier University.

11. Maselli, "People Problems."

Chapter 9

1. Schwartz, Karen D. (2001), *1to1 Magazine* (October), pp. 45-49.

2. Thompson, Toria (2001), "Data Puzzle," *1to1 Magazine* (July, August), pp. 47-50.

3. Downey, Bryant (2001), Presentation to Williams College of Business Administration MBA Class at Xavier University (April); "Executive Summary" (2001), *Consumer Goods Technology,* Supplement (April), pp. 4-7; "Future of CRM" (2000), *BusinessWeek* (July 3).

4. "Inventory to Visibility to Cut Inventories, Boost Customers Services" (2001), *Consumer Goods Technology,* Logistics Supplement, pp. 18-19.

5. Lawton, George (2001), "Nygard Stitches Knowledge into Business Processes," *Consumer Goods Technology* (October), pp. 11-12.

6. Andraski, Joseph C. (2001), "Progress and Opportunity," *Food Logistics and Retailtech* (Fall), pp. 6, 8-9.

7. Kioa, Kristen and Mariko Zapf (2001), "NAPM/Forrester Research Announce Results of Latest Report on eBusiness," <www.napm.org/NAPMReport/Forrester> (October 16).

8. Kurt Salmon Associates, Inc. (1993), *Efficient Consumer Response: Enhancing Consumer Value in the Grocery Industry,* Washington, DC: Food Marketing Institute.

9. Zimmerman, Kim Ann (2000), "Within Reach," *Food Logistics* (November/December), pp. 24-26; "The Culture of Collaboration—Part One" (2001), <www.ideabeat.com> (August 8).

10. Joachim, David and Chuck Moozakis (2001), "Can Covisint Find Its Way?", <Internetweek.com> (September 17).

11. "Up the Down Supply Chain" (2001), *Marketing News* (September 10), p. 3.

12. Ericson, Jim (2001), "Measuring Supplier Performance," <line56.com> (September 27).

13. Ericson, Jim (2001), "Measuring Supplier Performance," <line56.com> (September 26).

14. Kurt Salmon Associates, *Efficient Consumer Response.*

15. Karolefsky, John (2001), "Turning Chaos into Order," *Food Logistics and Retailtech* (Fall), p. 30.

16. Peck, Michael (2001), "CPFR: It Takes 2," *Consumer Goods Technology* (February), pp. 9-10.

17. Andraski, Joseph C. (2001), "Progress and Opportunity," *Food Logistics and Retailtech* (Fall), pp. 6, 8-9.

18. Peck, "CPFR: It Takes 2."

19. "Inventory Visibility to Cut Inventories, Boost Customer Service" (2001), *Consumer Goods Technology,* Logistics Supplement (May), pp. 18-20.

Chapter 10

1. "Bob Miller" (2001), *MMR* (September 17), p. 31.

2. Trottman, Melanie (2001), *The Wall Street Journal* (October 11), p. 1.

3. Terbeek, Glen (1999), *The Agentry Agenda: Selling Food in a Frictionless Marketplace.* Chesterfield, VA: The American Book Company.

4. Doherty, Katherine (1996), "Golden Cat in 'Pilot' Seat," *U.S. Distribution Journal* (May 15), p. 10.

5. Seybold, Patricia B., Ronni T. Marshak, and Jeffrey M. Lewis (2001), *The Customer Revolution,* New York: Crown Business.

6. Terbeek, *The Agentry Agenda.*

7. Perrotta, Peter (2001), "Giant Eagle Starts Private Exchange," *Supermarket News* (June 4), p. 45.

8. Seybold and Lewis, *The Customer Revolution.*

9. Terbeek, *The Agentry Agenda.*

10. Ewing, Jack (2000), "Siemens Climbs Back" (Int'l Edition), <www.businessweek.com> (June 5).

11. Seybold and Lewis, *The Customer Revolution.*

12. "Case Study: From Brochureware to Global eMarketing—Otis Elevator Revamps Its Site to Grow Sales and Save Costs," <us.f205.mail.yahoo.com> (September 25).

Index

For Product Safety Concerns and Information please contact our EU representative GPSR@taylorandfrancis.com Taylor & Francis Verlag GmbH, Kaufingerstraße 24, 80331 München, Germany

T - #0065 - 230425 - C0 - 212/152/16 - PB - 9780789015693 - Gloss Lamination